ECONOMIC DEVELOPMENT

WHAT EVERYONE NEEDS TO KNOW®

ECONOMIC DEVELOPMENT

WHAT EVERYONE NEEDS TO KNOW®

Second Edition

MARCELO M. GIUGALE

OXFORD
UNIVERSITY PRESS

OXFORD
UNIVERSITY PRESS

Oxford University Press is a department of the University of Oxford. It furthers
the University's objective of excellence in research, scholarship, and education
by publishing worldwide. Oxford is a registered trademark of Oxford University
Press in the UK and certain other countries.

"What Everyone Needs to Know" is a registered trademark
of Oxford University Press.

Published in the United States of America by Oxford University Press
198 Madison Avenue, New York, NY 10016, United States of America.

First Edition published in 2014
Second Edition published in 2017

CIP data is on file at the Library of Congress
ISBN 978-0-19-068842-4 (pbk.); 978-0-19-068841-7 (hbk.)

1 3 5 7 9 8 6 4 2

Paperback printed by WebCom, Inc., Canada
Hardback printed by Bridgeport National Bindery, Inc., United States of America

In Memory of Alicia Tamburelli . . . Gracias por todo, Vieja!

CONTENTS

3. Social Policy: Old War, New Weapons   66

4. Inclusion: Those Who Are Always Left Behind   89

PREFACE: WHOM IS THIS BOOK FOR?

Imagine that you want to get a feel for modern surgery. You may be an undergraduate student pondering medical school. Or a journalist researching a story about the new, cool things medicine can do. Or a politician trying to sound credible on healthcare reform. You may be one of those patients who wants to understand what the doctors are about to do to her. You could also be an experienced family physician who needs a quick refresher on the latest surgical techniques—which you may rarely practice. What is the best and fastest way to go about it? Simple: you get a friendly surgeon to lend you scrubs, take you inside the operating room, and let you witness a few actual operations. No lectures, no theories, no jargon—just a direct glance at the real thing. Well, that is in essence what this book does for those who are interested in economic development.

A series of short questions and answers, written in kitchen-table language, explain the issues that policymakers face, tell what the most promising instruments are in helping societies prosper, and show the limits of what we know. In fact, the idea is to get you to the frontier of the development profession, the point at which knowledge stops and ignorance starts, and to share with you what we don't know and make you think for yourself.

That frontier of knowledge changes all the time. Which is why this is the second edition of this book. The first was published in early 2014, and already much has been newly learned from practice. So I added twenty new questions and updated many of the answers to the questions we had before.

Like its predecessor, this second edition will have no master conceptual framework. There will be no formulae, tables, or charts either. Rather, we will *talk*, first about governments—after all, they are the ones who make decisions on policy—and about how they so frequently fail at what they do. We will then turn to the kind of economic policies without which no country can make it. Here is where technical orthodoxy will be translated into common sense—think about "macroeconomic consistency," "balanced budgets," and "monetary stability" as making ends meet for a country as a whole. From there, we will look at the excitement and the frustration that new tools and new realities are bringing to poverty reduction, social inclusion, education, health, technology, infrastructure, foreign aid—you name it. In the end, we will see all these tools in action in the region that represents development—and the need for it—better than any other: Africa. If, after all that, you are thirsty for more information, you will find a bibliography of suggested further readings. Some of them are classic, must-read books. Some are journal articles that changed the way economists think. And many are available online for free.

Three disclaimers before we go into the operating room. First, earlier versions of these essays have been published as blogs, opinion editorials, or both, in print or online. And I have tested the ideas in this book during dozens of lectures and speeches at universities in Africa, Asia, Europe, Latin America, and the United States. This allowed people to comment and allowed me to learn from those comments.

Second, I have spent the past twenty-seven years working for the World Bank, on four continents and in many capacities. There is no better institutional balcony from which to witness development—its actors, sectors, thinkers, places, lessons, and challenges. Still, the views conveyed here are my own, and they do not necessarily represent those of the World Bank or of the countries that own it. Third, I belong to no political party, commercial enterprise, interest group, or intellectual movement. So I am free to speak my mind.

Marcelo Giugale
Winter of 2017
@Marcelo_WB

ACKNOWLEDGMENTS

There are many colleagues in and around the profession whom I would like to thank for teaching me so much and for helping me make *Economic Development: What Everyone Needs to Know*® a reality. Omar Arias, Nancy Benjamin, Paul Brenton, Otaviano Canuto, Daniel Cotlear, Andrew Dabalen, David de Ferranti, Shantayanan Devarajan, Nora Dihel, Makhtar Diop, Bernard Funck, Ejaz Ghani, Swati Ghosh, Markus Goldstein, Faya Hayati, Fernando Im, Kai Kaiser, Olivier Lafourcade, Jan Loeprick, Gladys Lopez-Acevedo, Nga Thi Viet Nguyen, Margaret Miller, John Panzer, Remy Prud'homme, Anand Rajaram, Fernando Rojas, David Rosenblatt, Jaime Saavedra, Apurva Sanghi, Christopher Sheldon, Antoine Simonpietri, Mark Thomas, Volker Treichel, Jose Molinas Vega, Eduardo Velez, Jan Walliser, and Steve Webb either educated me in their respective fields or graciously invited me to comment on subjects they know much better than I.

Alex Fleming, Ellen Harvey, Michael Jelenic, and Susan Petersen encouraged me to see and tell the human story behind each technical issue, no matter how complex. Cristina Palarca and Patricia Mendez have over the years kept me organized in my day job, so I could spend nights, weekends, and airplane hours writing. And Angela

Chnapko, my publisher, saw the beauty—and took the risk—of bringing the trenches of the war on poverty to the hands and iPads of those who are not poor.

More personally, I am one lucky writer, blessed by the love and support of an incredible family. My kids—Carla, Lauren, and Juan—cheered me along and patiently put up with my passion for explaining things. And Pichu, my beloved wife of thirty-one years and my best friend, taught me that all problems in society really boil down to one solution: a good education. As a Special Ed teacher for some of the most special children there are, she should know.

To all, thank you.
Marcelo Giugale
Winter of 2017
@Marcelo_WB

ECONOMIC DEVELOPMENT

WHAT EVERYONE NEEDS TO KNOW®

OVERVIEW

WHAT IS ECONOMIC DEVELOPMENT AND WHAT DOES THIS BOOK SAY ABOUT IT?

At its most basic level, economic development is the process through which a community creates material wealth and uses it to improve the well-being of its members. This calls for many interrelated ingredients: healthy and educated workers, more machines and better infrastructure, advanced knowledge and pathbreaking ideas, savers and financiers, peace and the rule of law, and social inclusion and individual rights. The process can be helped or hindered by governments' policies and programs, so when it happens, it is usually associated with enlightened leaders. Note that economic development is more than a growing economy; you can have much of the latter but none of the former—for example, when the wealth that is created only benefits a small elite. That's why those who believe in economic development—this writer among them—also believe that poverty need not exist or persist.[1]

Technically, you are poor if you live on $3.10 a day or less. And if you live on less than $1.90—as almost 800 hundred million people do—you are "extremely poor." Those are the universal definitions of poverty, which economists use to make comparisons across countries.[2] Now, things can get more complicated. Each country also has its own official poverty line—the level of yearly income or consumption below which you are considered poor by your government. In 2015, the United States set that line at $11,770, implying that about 15 percent of Americans were poor. The broadly comparable figures for Nigeria were around $460 and 60 percent. In other words, being poor in Lagos is very different from being poor in Washington, DC. To add even more texture, many rightly argue that money is not all that counts in life. So additional dimensions are frequently added to the definition of poverty—how stable your income is, how included you feel in your society, how much opportunity your children have, how safe your neighborhood is, and how clean the air you breathe is.

When you finish reading this book, I hope you are convinced that economic development—and the reduction in poverty that goes with it—has never been more feasible for more countries. Mind you, there are huge risks behind that optimism. Big economies could fall into fiscal, financial, or confidence crises, and the effects could spill over to the rest of the world. Populist politicians may turn public opinion against globalization—the idea that, in the long run, we benefit from the free movement of goods, people, knowledge, and money. Natural disasters are more frequent and more catastrophic. And some places seem stuck in war. But the positive feeling of possibility, which permeates across issues, markets, sectors, policies, and nations, is real. It is inspired by a series of deep, simultaneous transformations that, slowly but surely, are changing the way we work, consume, save, and invest. Think of many tectonic plates shifting at the same time. What are those transformations?

First, the old relationship between "the state and the people" is becoming one between "the state and the person." Each of us will begin to have direct, individualized contact with our government. More and more of the things that the typical government gives to or does for its citizens—from public schooling to subsidized energy—will be turned into cash, delivered to you via cell phone or debit card. Even the national ownership of natural resources will gradually be redefined—just for being a citizen, you may one day get direct dividends from the companies that exploit your country's oil, gas, and minerals. The personalized relationship will not be just about money. It will also be about information. From your spending habits to your complaints about public services that don't work, your feedback will go directly to those who make decisions that affect you. Sound futuristic? Well, keep the idea in mind as you read through the chapters, and you'll see that it is already happening.

Second, the combination of more democracy and better data will make for smarter decisions, both by governments and by people. From finding the true impact—and the real beneficiaries—of public expenditures to controlling teacher absenteeism, and from fighting gender discrimination to facilitating cross-border trade, knowledge put in the hands of voters will translate into political pressure and, ultimately, reform. Information will not always and automatically lead to activism, though—not everyone has the time or the means for it. But aberrations that have survived for decades—like using taxpayers' money to pay for the gasoline consumed by the rich—will begin to crumble. Easy-to-understand "standards" will help us measure the performance of those who govern us. If the average second-grader cannot read at least sixty words per minute, there is something wrong with public education—*that's* a standard. And when public services like schools, hospitals, and the police fail, users no longer have to wait until the next election to punish the politician in office—they can shame him in an instant with a text, a tweet, or a post. All you need for this to happen is freedom of expression and the Internet. In fact, communication technology is speeding government accountability into real time.

Third, there will be no reason to leave anyone behind or disadvantaged. In a break from history, and thanks to better and cheaper identification technology, governments will know the poor by name, individually. Social assistance programs will be better tailored to their beneficiaries. This will reduce waste and increase impact. Blanket subsidies that benefit both rich and poor—say, selling electricity below cost for all houses—will disappear, saving money that can be then spent only on those in real need. Living on two dollars a day may indeed cease to be a relevant way to measure poverty, and other aspects of a good life may gain attention, like the risks you and your family face. And we will move away from the never-ending debate about equality of outcomes among adults—whether they should all earn and own the same—toward a consensus around equality of opportunity among children. Who can be against that?

Fourth, not only will citizens have better tools to change how governments behave, but the reverse will also be true. As hard evidence piles up on the role that culture plays in core development problems—from corruption and gender inequity to pollution and informality—new emphasis will be put on using public policy to change our values— those that make us think and act in a certain way. More countries will start to gather data on people's noncognitive skills—personality traits like conscientiousness, agreeableness, and extroversion—and to understand how those skills interact with cognitive ones—like IQ, test scores, or years of schooling. This could bring a major breakthrough in raising labor productivity: after all, employers pay more for workers who are both trained *and* trainable. One day, public education will balance teaching facts with teaching behaviors, knowledge with attitude.

Fifth, the main tenets of economic management are clear and broadly accepted. The global financial crisis of 2008–2009 and its long aftermath may have shaken some technical paradigms, especially about the wisdom of leaving bankers unchecked. A new wave of nationalism may have given us Brexit and bad-mouthed globalization. But sensible practitioners have not renounced the old religion of open economies, balanced budgets, independent central banks, low debt, good public institutions, smart regulation, lots of competition, and fair treatment of investors—big and small, local and foreign. Just remember this: economic growth is necessary but not sufficient for poverty to fall, and inflation is sufficient but not necessary for poverty to rise. People have understood that asymmetry: it has become more difficult for presidential candidates to win elections on a platform—or a brand—of fiscal mismanagement, rising prices, a stagnant economy, or frightened investors.

Sixth, the countries that will succeed—and many will—are those that will be able to balance economic discipline with social solidarity. Why should balancing efficiency with equity—markets with people, if you will—be the formula for success? Because it seems to align the entire society behind a broad, national vision—open for business *and* happy to pay so nobody, especially children, lacks the basics. This isolates economic development from wild political swings. Whether the Right or the Left comes to power becomes almost irrelevant. All that matters to voters is who is better at delivering the common vision.

Seventh, barring major surprises, Africa *will* finally make it. Yes, the continent looked promising many times before—and failed to take off. Much of its current shine is due to extractive industries like oil, gas, and minerals, whose international prices can—and do—swing widely. Not to mention the violent conflict that seems perennial in some of its countries. But Africa's emergence runs deeper. For one, the technologies for exploration and exploitation of its riches are getting cheaper, faster, and cleaner—many think that only one-tenth of its natural resources have been discovered. This time, the bonanza may be more about quantities than about prices. The spread of democracy is raising the quality of public policy among African governments—slowly, to be sure. The region's giant agricultural potential remains mostly untapped. And, in many areas, demography is beginning to show the benefits of slower population growth—fewer dependents per worker.

But, while all that is very exciting, nothing could transform and enrich Africa more than its self-integration. It remains a fragmented place, where people, goods, and capital can barely move from country to country, even between countries that have signed free trade agreements. Bureaucracy, overregulation, and monopolies make it almost impossible for African workers, traders, and financiers—except for the large and connected ones—to go where there is more demand for them. Those same barriers kill the possibility of forming the type of production chains that made East Asia so successful—where final products are assembled with components from many countries—so successful. They also kill the possibility that Africa can feed itself: it easily would, if food could circulate freely within the region. African nations usually say that their past was frustrated by how they were treated by outsiders—they are probably right on that. But how ironic is it that their future now depends on how they treat one another.

A final word before we jump into the chapters. From this overview, you may already get a sense that much can be done to bring people out of poverty. But you may also feel that in economic development there are few, if any, certainties. What works in one country may not work in another. You can spot broad trends but will always find outliers. There are no blueprints, and there is a lot of trial and error. It is as much about statistical sophistication as it is about plain common sense. And what we think we know today may melt in a flash of new technology tomorrow. Challenge, chance, and change. That's the beauty of this profession. Welcome.

1

GOVERNMENTS

ONE DAY, THEY WILL WORK FOR YOU

Why do obvious reforms never happen?

Case One. An African country spends 4 percent of its gross domestic product (GDP) every year paying for the gasoline consumed by its relatively few rich people. That would be enough money to *double* the budget for public education or *triple* the construction of hospitals—all services mostly used by the poor. One day the government decides to do something about this madness and tries to dismantle the gasoline subsidy. Social unrest follows. Who goes out to protest? The rich, right? After all, it is they who will lose the subsidy. No, actually the poor lead the demonstration.

Case Two. A Latin American government buys the television rights to the country's professional soccer league—yes, don't ask—and airs the games for free. Men—for in this country "futbol" is almost exclusively for them—are happy. Women hate it—their husbands will be glued to their TV sets all weekend long. Cost to the national treasury: about $250 million per year. This would be enough cash to give every child between the ages of two and five a preschool education, something that currently only well-to-do families can afford. Women would, of course, love that kind of childcare, not least because it would allow more of them to work outside the home. So, does the female vote in this country swing wildly against the party in office? Does the opposition even raise the possibility of trading soccer balls for children's cognitive development? Nope.

Case Three. A European country with massive unemployment decides to make it easier to hire and fire workers. The expectation—backed by pretty solid evidence—is that this will convince enterprises to recruit more, especially among the young. Labor unions, which are made up of people who *already* have jobs, strike in disgust. The government recoils, delays, and, finally, drops the reform. The unemployed do not get a chance to speak out.

Case Four. The most powerful government in the world runs a huge budget deficit and borrows to pay for it. That means that the current generation consumes more than it produces and passes the bill to the next generation in the form of larger national debt. Yes, some of today's expenditures are for things that will last a long time—like infrastructure. But most of the money goes to pay for tax breaks, free prescription drugs, and housing subsidies. Little of that benefits the young. Why are they not talking about it?

Case Five. A developed Asian economy restricts—and, at times, bans—the importation of rice, even though it is the staple food of its people. The end result is that consumers pay four times more for rice than they should. For the average family, that adds up to four hundred dollars per year of unnecessary expenditures, just to keep local rice farmers in business.

You see, all these cases are true stories. They are happening as we speak. And you can find hundreds more around the world. (Right now, you are probably thinking of one in your own country.) The losers in each case—the poor, the women, the unemployed, the young, the consumers—do not get organized to defend themselves. Somehow, societies tolerate these aberrations. They seem trapped in the status quo—a kind of low-level equilibrium that makes us collectively worse off. How come? Why is it that obvious reforms don't get done? Because behind every status quo, there is a complex cobweb of vested interests of people, institutions, and corporations—"actors"—who would be hurt by change, so they stop it. Economists call this interplay between losers, winners, and decision-makers, the "political economy" of reform—think of it as a power game played over economic policy.

There are, of course, ways to break the status quo. Crises are, ironically, among the most effective. It took a global financial meltdown in 2008 to get politicians everywhere to really focus on supervising banks, and it may take a natural disaster of cataclysmic proportions to get them to do something *together* about climate change. Not exactly a path to reform that you would wish on anyone.

Another way to break the impasse is through transformative leadership. Once in a while, societies find someone who inspires them, who is different, who can relate to people's present, and who can show them a vision of a better future. If you are lucky, that vision becomes actual progress. But, with inspirational leaders, you never know—off the top of your head, how many can you name that started well *and* ended well?

Perhaps technology is a more reliable, but still unpredictable, change-maker. An invention or a discovery can turn the political-economy game upside down. Mobile phones destroyed the dominant position of the old telephone companies. The Web is doing the same to once all-mighty newspapers. Drones will soon make fighter pilots look silly. And imagine what will happen to the clout of oil companies (and oil-rich countries) the day we figure out a cheaper way to fuel cars?

But if crises, leaders, and technology are just draws from a hat, is there a more systematic way to wake societies up? Yes: information. You see, most status quos are based on ignorance. When people find out how much money their governments waste or give to the rich, or the kind of privileges unions get, or how much cheaper imported stuff can be, their anger opens an opportunity for change. Opposition politicians—especially those who do not benefit themselves from the status quo—live off and tease that anger. Social outrage breaks out, and the game starts again until a new, hopefully better, equilibrium is reached. All you need is for knowledge to be put in the hands of ordinary people. Thank God for the Internet.

How is the relationship between the state and the citizen changing?

Over the past two decades, most developing countries (thirty-five of them in Africa alone) began to make direct cash transfers to their poor. Initially, this was meant to change the recipients' behavior—say, we give you money if you vaccinate your children. But this social policy tool is beginning to transform the way citizens relate to the state.

To start with, the logistics of the transfer are simple and getting cheaper. In most cases, a debit card or a cell phone is all you need. At each transaction, when the beneficiary spends the money, information is generated—on costs, preferences, impacts, needs. The accumulating data allows for better targeting, smarter design, less duplication, higher progressivity, closer monitoring, and more rigorous evaluation of social programs. You no longer have to second-guess people's needs; you can ask them directly. Your client is no longer "the people." It is the individual.

Of course, nothing prevents other public subsidies from being delivered in the same way. How about public services in general? And why use the direct-transfer technology only with the poor? Why not everybody? Let's work out a few examples to get a sense of the transformational power this would have.

Take tertiary education. Governments in Latin America, the Middle East, and other regions spend a fiscal fortune funding public universities. Most of their students are middle class or rich. And the quality of the education they get is mediocre at best. What would happen if the equivalent subsidy were provided directly to the students on their personal debit cards, for them to shop for colleges, public or private? Wouldn't good old public universities have to shape up? Wouldn't it then be easier to "means-test" the transfer, that is, to make it smaller for richer students? You get the point: by going directly to the individual you get a final outcome (education) that is better and fairer.

What works for education may also work for healthcare, for child nutrition, even for environmental protection. Rather than paying for public hospitals, with their ongoing problems and poor service, couldn't you transfer the money to each citizen so they can choose a health provider? And can't you load the debit cards of indigent mothers with money for baby formula or vitamins? Or the cell phones of farmers with credits to pay for professional pest control, if they can't afford it?

The new relationship does not stop at handouts from the state to the citizen. It involves information—and trust—too. Wouldn't you want to know how much money your government gets from the companies that exploit your country's oil, gas, or minerals? It doesn't have to be exact, but a ballpark figure. And how about taking a peek at the contracts that your leaders sign on your behalf (remember, you and your fellow citizens are the real owners of your national wealth)? And aren't you curious about where the money goes—or went? It is a bit of a puzzle that, by the end of 2015, only 31 out of 196 countries in the world complied with the requirements of the Extractive Industries Transparency Initiative (EITI), an invitation dating back to 2003 to publish who pays how much to whom in the business of exploiting natural resources.[1] Of those thirty-one, only one (Norway) can be considered "developed," and eighteen are African. Yes, this transparency makes life less comfortable for foreign corporations and for the politicians that grant them concessions. That's exactly the point.

Finally, the mechanisms used to transfer money in one direction can also be used to transfer information in the opposite one. For example, governments could pay people to fill out household surveys through their cell phones. Some of this is already happening (pilot experiments are being carried out in Cameroon, Malawi, and Senegal). It is increasing not just the knowledge the state has of each citizen, but the frequency of information too. It will soon allow us to answer in real time questions that, until now, took months, if not years, to answer, for example: What jobs exactly did the global crisis destroy? How are rising food prices affecting families? Why do people migrate? Are teenagers quitting high school? Why is polio coming back? All this will help governments respond in more timely and more meaningful ways.

Needless to say, none of the above will happen overnight. The vested interests in the state-as-we-know-it are many. This is true not only in developing countries—try to reform Europe's public universities, for instance—and there will be actual supply constraints—what do you with a loaded debit card if your village has no hospital or electricity for that matter? But the ballooning expansion, and collapsing cost, of communications technology even in the least developed parts of the world will put most of us in a direct relationship with our governments.

Why should governments intervene in markets?

It was 2007. The world of finance was booming. Even people with bad or no credit history could borrow money to buy a house, see it gain value, sell it, and make a quick profit. "Subprime mortgage," "bullet repayment," and "house flipping" were part of the middle-class vernacular. Somehow, Wall Street bankers had found a way to "package and slice" these loans and make them riskless. Well, we all know how that ended. What we don't know is how we—as a society—believed that the magic would last and went along with it. Think about buying a car or house too big for you, or paying outrageous interest on your credit card just to wear designer labels, or playing slot machines designed to beat you, or eating things proven to damage your health? Why do we, rational as we think we are, fall for all this?

Because markets are full of swindlers-in-waiting who talk directly to the "bad monkey" that each of us carries on our shoulders—that is, to the part of our self that is driven by emotion or biases, not reason. With only a bit of oversimplification, that is the main message of a 2015 book called *Phishing for Phools: The Economics of Manipulation & Deception.* Before you roll your eyes, you should know that the two authors of this book, George Akerlof and Robert Shiller, are both Nobel laureates and, frankly, rank among the most respected economists alive. What are these two academics up to?

A lot. They combed through tons of evidence from social psychology, behavioral economics, and industrial history to show example after example of how humans are fundamentally weak—we can be duped into doing things that we *know* are not in our best interest. All it takes for us to succumb to our lower material instincts is manipulated information delivered through smart marketing—aka "phishing." In a free market, sellers try to sell as much as they can by whatever means they can—including, if nothing stops them, phishing. If they didn't, someone else would, which would drive them out of business. Competition ensures that if we can be "phished," we will. It is, in technical parlance, a market equilibrium.

So, to keep us safe from the "phishers," governments need to intervene and regulate the market—at least to curb the most blatant excesses. This is why public agencies like the Securities and Exchange Commission, the Food and Drug Administration, or the Bureau of Consumer Protection exist. It is also what many private organizations try to do—from those that provide us consumer reports to those that warn us against blood diamonds. Akerlof and Shiller rightly call these people heroes.

Of course, all of this is borderline blasphemy to those who believe markets work best when people are "free to choose"—as Milton Friedman, another Nobel laureate and legend of economics, put it thirty-five years ago. Leave them alone, and consumers will learn from their mistakes and begin to shun dishonest sellers. Over time, reputations will matter. You need no government intervention. After all, what do bureaucrats know about business? Regulators are no match for the likes of Enron and Bernie Madoff, anyway. And why should a civil servant choose for me? As you can see, this conversation can get very ideological.

But, ideology aside, there are two aspects of Akerlof and Shiller's view of markets that make you scratch your head.

First, it smacks of a rich man's problem. Their examples, and their hinted solutions, fit developed countries, especially the United States, well. But they seem a lot less relevant to the developing world. When you live on two dollars a day or less, as almost one billion human beings currently do, you cannot afford to listen to the monkey on your shoulder. Almost all your income goes to food. There is no freedom to choose, simply because there is no money to choose with. Period. When living in misery, you *want* government intervention, not so much to scare off potential phishers, but to give you whatever help it can. The key word here is "can." Among poor countries, not all governments have the capacity to provide basic nutrition, education, and healthcare, and to regulate markets. What do you do then?

Second, one would suspect that generations get smarter—or are at least better informed—over time. Progress in educational attainment, access to information, and social activism ought to count for something—our monkey is not the same monkey that our grandparents carried. Today, a tweet, a post, or a blog is enough to alert millions in seconds of a dreadful restaurant, an unsafe toy, or a polluting car company. We can share our market experiences in real time. This narrows the space for phishing.

Still, the flaws of governments and the spread of the Internet do not invalidate the central point of this book: our veneration of free markets—and, its counterpart, our distrust of government—assumes that buyers *always* know what they want and sellers are *always* honest. Recent evidence has proven that assumption to be, at best, naive. And we, as individuals and as societies, pay a huge price for our naiveté—in terms of financial instability, healthcare costs, environmental degradation, and many others. Economic freedom, it turns out, is not free.

Has government decentralization worked?

Think back to the 1990s. The Soviet Union had just disintegrated. The American economy was on a roll. Technology and the Internet were starting to connect people. And democracy was spreading fast, especially among developing countries that never had it before. The headlines were about fresh new presidents and voters speaking up freely. Behind the headlines, a subtler political change was taking place: power was beginning to shift from central governments to states and municipalities. Vital public services for the common citizen—like education, healthcare, water, electricity, and many others—were becoming the responsibility of governors and mayors. With this responsibility came money, some through transfers from the national budget, some in new local taxes, and some from lenders eager to gain new clients. These were the times of "decentralization," the catchy idea that closer proximity—literally—between those who govern and those who are governed is always a good thing. No one could ever know people's preferences better than their local authorities, right? And if local leaders failed to deliver, it would be easier for you to hold them accountable—after all, they are more likely to be your neighbors. This would surely improve service, reduce corruption, and save money. Case closed. So countries decentralized fast and furious.

Twenty years later, it is fair to ask: Has decentralization worked? Well, the answer is a bit anticlimactic. When it was done well, decentralization did work. Success only came with smart design and careful implementation. You see, decentralization was—and still is—a high-risk, high-reward reform. A lot can go wrong with it. Local bureaucracies may not have the capacity to manage a school system or a power-distribution network. They may not have the "scale" to keep costs down—you can negotiate better prices for, say, trash collection trucks if you buy them by the thousands for a country rather than by the dozen for a county. Small-town politicians may be easier to lobby—or to bribe. Labor disputes, obsolete equipment, and irresponsible pension promises are just some of the problems that usually plague the public services that get decentralized— federal governments are only too happy to see someone else blamed. Left to fend for themselves, remote poor areas may become even poorer, while big cities close to ports grow bigger and richer—this is when geography begins to matter and regional resentment begins to fester.[2] Then there is the "bailout" issue: What should the central government do if a local government goes bankrupt? Can it watch and do nothing as a province's children go without school and its hospitals go without power? South America is living proof that, when that happens, "the federation" has no choice but to step in and pay up—which, in effect, means that everyone in the nation pays up too.[3]

With that much risk at play, it is not surprising that few countries can claim success in decentralization. In fact, there is no evidence that when the government is more decentralized, the economy grows faster or is more stable—there is not enough data to tell one way or the other.[4] Nor is it clear that more power to local governments automatically translates into less poverty.[5] What we have is a growing inventory of experiences from around the world that show how specific public services improved— sometimes a lot—when local authorities began to run them. For example, giving Swiss cantons control over education raised student test scores. In Canada, infant mortality fell faster when provinces were made responsible for it. The same happened among Spain's poorest regions.[6] Bolivian municipalities managed to invest more in water and sanitation where it was most needed, something that translated into healthier local populations.[7] Enrollment in Ethiopia's primary schools shot up when woredas—a type of territorial division somewhere between a neighborhood and a municipality—were put in charge.[8] The list goes on.

But you can build a similar list with public services that *deteriorated* when they were decentralized. So, the real question is not whether decentralization has worked or not, but whether there is something in common among the cases where it has. There is. First, decentralization makes innovation easier. It seems that governors and mayors manage to experiment with new ways to deliver old services. Take the case of schools in Bogotá, Colombia. The city wanted to improve its education system. It hired some of the best and most exclusive private schools to run twenty-five of its own establishments in low-income areas. Students in these "concession" schools—where the power of teacher unions was limited—did much better on standardized tests than their peers in the rest of the public system. (Many actually scored higher than their peers in the parent private school!) It would have been politically and practically impossible for the central government to try something like that in the country as a whole.

Second, technology helps decentralization. In the past two decades, computers, cell phones, and the Web have made it easier to control and to provide public services at the local level. Training of municipal officials can now be done online. They have access to the same information as big bureaucracies in the capital city. They can learn from each other with a click of a mouse. New gadgets like transponders, remote meters, and bar codes have made it simpler to charge for highways, water, and licenses. And Twitter, Facebook, and YouTube can be used to embarrass the mayor if he is caught red-handed or the local electricity company if it fails to restore power fast enough or the city's sheriff if he keeps pulling over drivers always of the same skin color. New technology provides instant accountability at the tip of the neighborhood's fingers.

And third, debt has to be kept low. Over time, local governments developed their own sources of income. Many began to receive large transfers from their countries' sales of oil, gas, and minerals. This made them more creditworthy. Bankers started to offer them loans. Governors and mayors who avoided—or were not allowed to engage in—borrowing binges did better than those who didn't. Why? Because paying off hefty debts meant less funding for schools, hospitals, and roads. The alternative was, of course, to beg for money from the federal government in exchange for political favors—a very messy alternative. Not surprisingly, central governments have tried to ban or at least control "subnational" borrowing, with mixed results. (If you are looking for a good way to regulate this, check what Mexico did: they made banks set aside larger loan provisions when they lent to subnationals with low credit ratings.[9])

So, if decentralization needs such careful fine-tuning to work well, why do it at all? Because it's what people want. We like to choose our local leaders and to have a voice in the services we use day in and day out. There is no going back on that. The genie of decentralization is out of the bottle. By now, in the average developing country, states and municipalities are in charge of one-fifth of all public expenditures. That proportion is above one-third in places like Argentina, India, Russia, and South Africa. It will continue to grow. That's why the next time there are local elections where you live, be sure to vote.[10]

Do we really care about graft?

What makes a middle-class, middle-aged, Middle Eastern mother risk her life, liberty, and livelihood to join street demonstrators and stand up against a mighty ruler? Think about it. Behind the masses in Cairo's streets and elsewhere during the spring of 2011, there was a moment of personal decision. Something tips your scale toward involvement. Something finally makes you act. Suddenly, having your government accountable to you—and not the other way around—is worth putting it all on the line. It reaches the top of your value list.

But what if that change in values—that cultural change—could take place as part of a society's normal evolution rather than by revolution? Could people be taught to relish public accountability? Can the demand for "good governance" be created or, at least, fostered? These are critical questions for developing countries, which cannot afford bad governments. For them, mistaken or corrupt policies usually mean more poverty and the immediate suffering that accompanies it.

We know surprisingly little about how to make people value good government. There are, however, plenty of hypotheses—and some experiments. First hypothesis: it's about kindergartens. Like any other change in culture, you start by teaching little kids. This, of course, has been used for good (e.g., Greenpeace) and for evil (e.g., Hitler). But it works. The problem is that it takes a generation, and it is not cheap (to start with, you have to have a functioning school system). In the developing world, Mexico pioneered some of this in its fight against petty corruption through the *"No Más Mordidas!"* campaign, which focused its anti-graft efforts on educating school-age children.

Second hypothesis: it's about money. If you want citizens to care about how their government manages resources, give them a direct stake. Imagine if a percentage of the profits of a national oil company were transferred directly to every resident, no questions asked. What do you think would happen with public interest in and scrutiny over the company's performance and transparency? There would be instant demand for accountability—if it didn't find and sell oil, you would personally lose money. Now picture the same mechanism applied to Africa's bountiful extractive industries, from diamonds to gold to timber. (Prediction: in ten years, this kind of direct dividend transfers will be common practice.)

Third hypothesis: it's about connectivity. That the Internet, social media, and smart phones help people act collectively is indisputable. But having the means to hold your government accountable is different from actually holding it accountable. When was the last time you visited the website of your country's ministry of finance to check on the execution of the budget? Or tweeted about the lack of investment in public infrastructure? Do you know the name of your minister of education, the one that makes policy regarding your children's learning? The good news here comes from Africa: its citizens are embracing cellular phones with gusto and are using them to report on public services—or lack thereof. In parts of rural Tanzania, parents have been given phones to report teachers who do not show up at school. Teachers unions hate this, which is the whole point, but teacher absenteeism has fallen dramatically.

Fourth hypothesis: it's about free media. We tend to care about the news we hear about most often. And poor governance is rarely breaking news; in fact, the deterioration in public accountability is usually a slow, imperceptible decline. But think again. Over the past decade or so, international nongovernmental organizations (NGOs) have managed to produce indices that benchmark governments against one another. When Transparency International publishes its annual Corruption Perception Index, journalists have a field day telling us how bad our country compares with our neighbors'.[11] Ditto when the Organization for Economic Cooperation and Development (OECD) puts out the results of its triannual Program for International

Student Assessment—that's the week when we all talk about how East Asians are leaving (almost) everybody else in the educational dust. There are plenty more examples— indices that tell us how competitive, polluted, democratic, developed, or fair our nations really are. The news, especially when it is bad news, can prod us to demand performance from those who lead us. This is accountability by global name-and-shame.

Fifth hypothesis: it's about institutions. You need certain tools to make your demand for public accountability stick. The most obvious is access to information, and the laws that make it possible. You need technical agencies that can independently interpret the data for you—those think tanks, congressional budget offices, and ombudsman services are the best allies of the layperson. And you need a court that will hear your complaints. That's where accessible judicial systems come in. Are all these institutional tools available to the average citizen in the developing world? No. But they are getting better, as societies become more open. Take the case of Ghana: in 2011, its parliament passed legislation giving civil society a direct-view balcony on how oil and gas contracts and revenues will be managed. Others are now doing the same. Respect to them.

Which brings us to the sixth and final hypothesis: it's about democracy. If you lack basic civil liberties, if your freedom to vote or to speak is taken away, calling for accountability from public officials may be difficult— and outright dangerous. But isn't that the message from that middle-aged woman in Cairo? Isn't she saying that even if you ignore her children's education, squander her resources, shut down the Web, silence the media, and manipulate institutions, she will one day risk it all and go out to demand good governance? In other words, bad governments don't last forever in any culture.

Why can't we stop conflict?

In 2011, the World Bank published its annual *World Development Report* (*WDR*), something it has been doing for more than three decades.[12] (Disclosure: this economist has been contributing comments to early drafts of the *WDR* for the past twenty-seven years.) That year's volume is about security and development. It says that societies are constantly under internal and external "stresses" such as corruption, youth unemployment, racial discrimination, religious competition, foreign invasion, and international terrorism.

Those stresses can become violent conflicts if we lack the "institutions" to manage them. A typical institution is an independent judiciary, an elected parliament, or a police force. When those are bad or bent, not only are people more likely to engage in conflict, but they are also more likely to go at each other over and over again—conflict becomes a repetitive trap.

So the big question is not just how to stop violence but also how to avoid its recurrence. Finding an answer is urgent, not least because the cost of conflict is huge—on average, it sets an economy back thirty years and sends one-fifth of its population into poverty. Add to that the loss of life, the psychological trauma, and the lasting social rancor. One in four human beings currently lives in a violent place.

The report proposes a rather predictable solution to break the cycle of violence: we need better institutions. This is as true for, say, Africa's Sahel today as it was for Europe after World War II. But what does it actually mean for people? In practice, what are the "institutions" that matter to each of us?

Take the case of the eighty-year-old grandmother who stepped out of her church in a working-class neighborhood.

Two teenagers came up to her, pulled her purse out of her hands, tore off her necklace, knocked her to the ground, and ran away. She stood up and, trembling, walked home. It never crossed her mind to report the assault to the police—she knew better. Question: In the eyes of this lady, which institution failed? Who neglected to protect her community, educate her attackers, and inspire her trust in justice?

Now scale the case up. A gang of drug traffickers enters a disco at a border city during a birthday party, shoots dead everyone inside, and leaves. A warlord sends his twelve-year-old soldiers to massacre an entire village that happens to be located close to a diamond mine. A president is unseated by popular vote but refuses to accept the election's outcome, unleashing a wave of terror on his opponents. A charismatic university professor convinces poor peasants that their poverty will go away if they just eliminate anyone who is not poor like them. In all these cases, institutions failed the victims of violence—the state, the market, the army, the education system, the media, the international community, none of them did what they were supposed to.

Which brings us back to the 2011 *WDR*. It says that we can build institutions good enough and legitimate enough not just to prevent violent conflict but also to avoid falling back into it. It suggests some quick wins—things like firing crooked officials, publishing the budget, scrapping discriminatory laws, and dismantling secret police forces. It also points out some long-term reforms: build a fair judiciary, let local communities administer schools, prioritize job creation among the young, and so on. But behind all these proposals there is a common element: institutions are good and legitimate only if people can trust them. And the only way to create trust is through results.

In the eye of the common citizen, the police will be "good" when the streets are safe; the schools will be "good" when children attend, learn, and graduate; and the electoral commission will be "good" when it shows independence. Yes, measuring safety, educational achievement, or political freedom is technically much more difficult than it sounds.[13] But you get the point: institutions are about confidence, and confidence is about performance. That is the essence of the social contract that makes peace, and thus development, possible.

Are natural resources a curse?

The evidence is as strong as it is puzzling: countries that have a lot of natural resources—things like oil, gas, and minerals—tend to be poorer than those that don't. Over time, they grow slower, become less competitive and innovative, and suffer from more corruption and pollution. No wonder many say that "commodity wealth" is actually a curse. If it is, then we have a serious problem. The rents generated by extractive industries are growing super-fast and, by now, are worth some five trillion dollars per year—that's almost one-tenth of the annual value of all goods and services produced by the entire planet. And most of that money is going to developing countries—especially Africa—where it has the potential to cause the most "damage."

Of course, if you ask economists, they'll tell you that they have already figured out ways to turn this curse into a blessing. They know what central banks need to do to keep the local currency from appreciating beyond the point at which our noncommodity industries are destroyed by cheaper imports. (The appreciation, of course, happens because exporting commodities brings lot of foreign currency, usually US dollars, into the economy.) They also speak of "fiscal rules," "multiyear budgets," and "sovereign wealth funds"—all things that act like speed bumps so governments don't waste the commodity money too quickly. They have techniques to make public spending, especially investments in infrastructure, a bit more productive (mostly through smart project design, implementation, and evaluation). And they have teamed up with NGOs, think tanks, academia, credit-rating agencies, and even churches to insist that exploration, exploitation, and expenditures are as clean and as green as possible.

So, if we know exactly what to do to avoid the commodity curse, then why doesn't it get done? Why, in spite of bad experience after bad experience, of libraries full of technical ideas, and of warning calls from all corners of society, do most countries endowed with natural wealth end up wasting it? A 2012 book—*Rents to Riches?*—looks around the world and concludes that the culprit lies in "political economy," that is, in the interplay of vested interests that smothers reform.[14] Here is how it happens, as well as a few hints at a solution.

First, you have to convince investors—especially foreign ones—to explore your land, and if they find something valuable, to extract it, ship it out, and give you a cut. They will have to put huge amounts of cash up front—the average, deep-water oil well costs about one hundred million dollars to drill and has a one-in-ten chance of succeeding. How do those investors know that, once they find something, you will not break the contract and tax their rents away? You see, "contractual security" is the first consideration in the extractive business. Think of a gas pipeline or an oil platform: What happens if, a few years after you build it, a radical politician comes into office and wants to expropriate it? Will you be able to defend your rights in court? Whose court? That kind of credibility is crucial. The less you can trust a country's political and legal systems, the larger the share of the discoveries you will demand to take the investment risk in the first place.

Second, the citizens need to be convinced. They will support the sale of natural resources only if they feel that they, not corrupt officials, will benefit from it—if they feel "included" in the deal. Such inclusion means governments spend the commodity revenue well—on "public goods" like primary education, basic healthcare, and safety. It also means opening access to information, auctioning extraction rights in a transparent way, and holding public officials accountable for the results they achieve—or don't achieve. Rarely would all that happen in undemocratic countries.

So, if your country is politically stable and socially inclusive, then it is possible to reach consensus on what needs to be done to turn commodities into a blessing (best example: Norway). Whether it is managing the currency, monitoring the budget, or protecting the environment, stability and inclusion make things much easier to agree on. But what do you do when your leaders keep changing through violence and your people think extractive industries are a scam that favors only the elite? That's when you are likely to see concessions that smack of giveaways, politicians who seem to take turns enriching themselves, little or no economic development, and citizens who hate it all. What do you do in that case?

Well, you can improve at the edges. The international community can put pressure on countries and corporations to get all concession agreements disclosed, to make contracts as standard as possible, and to get independent parties to monitor them (here is where reputable experts, academics, and NGOs can be useful). You can make the government's share of the rents increase automatically when prices balloon—so old contracts don't look like sweetheart deals at times of bonanza. You can make public investment as professional and as decentralized as possible. You can form coalitions of the interested: help civil society get organized and have a say about the whole process, especially around the locations where mines, wells, and pipelines will be constructed (the Ambatovy nickel mine in Madagascar is a fairly good example of this).

If all that fails, you can always do the unthinkable: give citizens a direct stake in their own national resources. The biometric and logistical tools (think of iris scanners and debit cards) to transfer a portion of commodity rents to every man, woman, and child already exist; in fact, the cost of identifying and reaching individuals has collapsed over the past decade. This would make people really interested in how the government spends the rents that it does *not* transfer. They would begin to care more about how well the industry is managed than about the nationality of whoever manages it. And they would definitely feel "included." Will this just foster private consumption at the expense of public investment? Not necessarily. If the new scrutiny reduces corruption, you may end up with more money than before to build ports, bridges, and power plants. Sure, developing countries are not Alaska, where this kind of transfer has been common practice for decades (the Alaska Permanent Fund, established in 1976, accumulates a portion of the state's annual oil revenues, and every year distributes a dividend of about a thousand dollars to each resident of the state).[15] But with so much at stake in the coming years, the idea is certainly worth a try.

What are the signs a country is managing its riches well?

Say that your country is blessed with natural resources. Oil, gas, minerals—it has it all. New technologies are leading to even more discoveries. Your president is on television on an almost daily basis signing new exploration deals—likely with foreign companies—or happily announcing new finds. The future looks good. But deep down you worry that the bonanza could turn into a bust—maybe you live in Africa and have seen how windfalls have been wasted before. How do you know that's not going to happen now? Are there any telltale signs of sound management of "commodity wealth"? In fact, there are six.

First, the government publishes the contracts it signs with the companies that are given the right to explore, exploit, and export. The idea is both to set an early tone of transparency around the whole business of extraction and, more important, to force public officials to develop enough negotiating and regulatory capacity of their own— lest they be accused of incompetence or, worse, corruption. It seems simple enough, but not every country—rich or poor—discloses those contracts.[16]

Second, the price projections used to construct the government's budget are calculated by someone outside government (usually reputable experts and academics). This is critical. The budget is like an annual authorization to spend. How much you spend depends on how much revenue you believe you will have, which in turn depends on what prices you think you will get for the commodities you export. Politicians tend to be grossly overoptimistic about those prices, because they always want to spend as much as possible on their constituencies. So, having an independent, technical, above-the-fray party calling or, at least, vetting the commodity prices on which the budget is based is a great sign of discipline. Not many countries do it—at least not yet—but the few that do are seen as examples of good management (Chile comes to mind).

Third, some—even a little—of the rent from the exploitation of natural resources is saved. The money is put away in a "sovereign wealth fund," presumably to be used during bad times or by future generations. This is not only a powerful sign of fiscal prudence, but it also helps keep society's attention on the extractive industry—the media would have pointy questions if the fund suddenly stopped growing or shrank. Since 1990 the number of countries that have built these funds has tripled—to more than forty—and, together, they hold about seven *trillion* dollars, the majority of which came from the sale of commodities. There are good examples among emerging economies: Azerbaijan, Chile, and Trinidad and Tobago. And good examples among developed countries: Australia, Norway, and Singapore.[17]

Fourth, the stock of public debt is falling. This is, of course, equivalent to accumulating revenues in a sovereign wealth fund. Paying down government debt is like a transfer of the commodity wealth to the young—when they start working, they won't have to be taxed so heavily. You should worry if you see your country quickly depleting its oil or gold deposits *and* borrowing fast at the same time—not an unusual sight, unfortunately.

Fifth, the evaluation of public investment projects is done by a team of professionals. This team sits at the office in the ministry of finance or planning charged with making sense of the hundreds of project proposals generated by other parts of the government—and with advising on which ones to pay for and which ones to drop. They need to know the ins and outs of almost every sector, from education to agriculture to transport. And, naturally, they are under enormous political pressure. The good ones try to frame their views as "result contracts" (what exactly is going to be achieved with each investment?) and are champions at distilling lessons from the past (what exactly was achieved with the money already spent?).

And sixth, the government's final accounts for the year—the execution of the budget, if you will—are audited on time, and the results are made public. (Question: Can you name your country's auditor general—aka "comptroller general"—the person who is supposed to keep your leaders honest?) For many a developing country, because of negligence, incompetence, political interference, or outright corruption, those audits are usually incomplete or late, which renders every other fiscal precaution meaningless— if nobody checks whether the approved budget is *actually* respected, there is little point in having a budget to start with.

Contracts, prices, savings, debts, investments, and audits—six ways to know when things are working fine. But if that's too much information for the average citizen to obtain, there is one other, less technical behavior that sets apart countries that manage their natural wealth prudently: they treat it as if it belonged to their children. Imagine that your kids receive a large inheritance for which you are the trustee. Would you spend it on your own consumption? Would you borrow against it? Or would you use part of it to give them a better education, good healthcare, physical security, and a decent place to live, and save the rest for them to decide what to do with it when they grow up? We know the right answer to that. Well, what's true for our families is true for our countries too.

2

ECONOMIC POLICY

THE BASICS YOU'VE GOT TO GET RIGHT

Why do governments struggle to prop up the world's economy?

"Out of ammo," "helicopter money," "monetary impotence," "infrastructure push," "savings glut." These are the kind of strange handles economists use when debating why the world's economy has been stuck since the great recession of 2008–2009 and what governments should do to jolt it out of its lethargy. The data is clear. Growth in global output has declined to about half what it was before 2008. Nobody expects this trend to improve much before the end of the decade, and the blues have spared almost no country. From Europe to Japan, and from China to Brazil, economic growth is flat, falling, or failing. Why can't policymakers do something about it?

To be fair, they have been trying. But the old weapons don't seem to work anymore. Central banks, especially in rich countries, have reduced interest rates all the way down to zero—and, in some cases, even below zero—in a sensible attempt to make credit cheaper. But it turns out that there were not enough investors and consumers willing to take on more credit. Those same central banks then opted for their equivalent of heavy weaponry and began to trade bonds for cash—aka "quantitative easing." That helped, but not much. And since 2016, they have been seriously considering a nuclear option: just printing money and giving it to the government to spend. They hope that some more public infrastructure here or a tax cut there can spur the economy. You get a sense of what "helicopter money" means.

What's happening? In a nutshell, the world is saving too much and investing too little. This is not new. It has been in the making for the past quarter century. The telling symptom that there is a yawning gap between how much we save and how much we invest is in the price of savings, that is, in the interest rates we pay for loans. Controlling for inflation, those rates have been on the decline since the early 1990s. In a 2015 research paper, Lukasz Rachel and Thomas Smith, two economists at the Bank of England, show that, on average, long-term real interest rates in advanced economies have fallen by more than 4 percentage points—that's a lot, as anyone who has ever had a mortgage will tell you.[1]

More to the point, when you look at its probable causes, the chasm between saving and investment shows no signs of closing. Rising income inequality, aging populations, and lack of trust in government have all played a role. Because they lack for little, the rich save a larger proportion of their income compared with the poor. So do those of working age, compared with the young and the old. And, when the price of commodities was booming, many countries blessed with oil, gas, or minerals set up "sovereign wealth funds" to put away some of the windfall for a rainy day, just to make sure that politicians did not squander it.

On the investment side, things are less obvious. Nobody knows for sure what has been restraining it all these years.

Some point to the steep fall in the price of capital goods, like cranes or computers—they say that when projects get cheaper, investors do not necessarily do more projects. Others blame it on a protracted retrenchment of public investment since the early 1980s, driven mostly by ideology. Governments in the industrial world are estimated to have cut back on capital expenditures, on average, by 1 percent of GDP—not minor, if you consider that their level of investment stands at about 3 percent of GDP. These changes in both private and public attitudes toward investment could not come at a worse time, as no one expects the world economy to recover its turbo-charged growth of the 1990s. Short of a game-changing technology suddenly raising our productivity—like the Internet did—long-term global growth will stay modest at best. Why invest if business will be soft?

So, the world may need to get used to super-low interest rates. Is that really a problem? It certainly makes life more difficult for central bankers. They cannot be counted on to smooth downturns in the economy. But some will argue that the time has never been better for governments to borrow as much as they need to build first-class infrastructure. This should boost the economy now—welcome to the "infrastructure push"—and in the future: better ports, roads, and power grids should make us all more productive. Others scratch their heads at the idea of giving a blank check to politicians. It can forever shatter any sense of fiscal discipline, and it assumes that civil servants have the capacity to get projects done fast enough. Fair worries.

But, if central banks are "impotent" and governments must be kept on a leash, how do we break the saving-investment conundrum? The answer, in two words, is "structural reform." This is old religion among economists—well known, hard, glamour-less. But it works. It simply means making life easier for investors, big and small, foreign and local. It involves basic virtues like open trade, smart regulation, reasonable taxes, skillful workers, secure contracts, accessible land, and reliable logistics. Maybe, just maybe, in a world where cheap loans alone fail to entice entrepreneurs, we should look at what else is holding them back and fix it.

What is structural reform?

It is late 2016. All indicators point to a world economy that will remain weak next year and in the longer term, in advanced and developing countries alike. Governments are feeling the pressure from voters to deliver faster economic growth—and plenty of jobs. Discontent is spreading and is threatening globalization. Urgent action is needed. But the truth is that policymakers are trapped between two unprecedented realities. The first is that the monetary and fiscal tools they have to manage their way out of short-term slumps are no longer effective or available—interest rates are already at almost zero and can't be cut much more, and there is no political appetite to let politicians borrow more to spend more. The second reality has to do with economic growth itself: it is becoming less dependent on accumulating capital and labor, more connected across borders, more urban, more private, and more volatile—that is, more complex.

So the search is on for a way to deal with *both* the cyclical downturn and the new nature of growth. Enter "structural reform," a broad label for any change in laws, regulations, policies, institutions, and logistics that makes investing more attractive and more profitable—whatever the level of interest rates. This is the advice of mainstream economists, whether for China, Brazil, Europe, Japan, or South Africa. It is also a public commitment of the "G20," the forum that brings together the political leaders of the world's largest economies. And it is a loud and recurrent request at the World Economic Forum, the prime advocacy platform for the global business community.

The concept is not new. Structural reform, aka "structural adjustment," was en vogue in the late 1980s and early 1990s as a means to rescue debt-burdened developing countries. It involved policies like privatization of public enterprises, the elimination of subsidies, the reduction of import tariffs, and widespread deregulation. This market-friendly mix became known as the "Washington Consensus" because it was the staple recommendation of the International Monetary Fund (IMF) and the World Bank. Many countries had no choice but to accept the recommendation, so it got a bad rap. Interestingly, almost three decades later, it is back in fashion.

But, what structural reforms should a government choose? It depends on the country. Think of the health of an economy as the health of a human being. You know the marks of a healthy person: a body mass index of 22, a resting heart rate of 50 beats per minute, a total cholesterol level under 200 mg/dl, a blood sugar count at dawn of 100 mg/dl or less, and so on. How you *get to* those marks depends on where you *start from*. If you are young, slim, and athletic, small adjustments to your lifestyle may do the trick. If you are an old, obese, sedentary, smoking heavy-drinker, a major program of diet, exercise, behaviors, and medicines may be called for—at once! The same case-by-case specificity applies to economies and structural reforms. There is no blueprint. Still, experience suggests a few guiding principles.

The first of those principles is that the lower a country's income level, the more critical it is to get the basics right. Reforms that, say, let farmers in low-income countries profit from their crops or own their land have a much larger impact on growth than making business or patent registration faster. For their part, highly industrialized economies might be held back by labor regulations, but these barely apply in places where employment through formal contracts is rare.

Second, how reforms are sequenced, how they are grouped, and at what moment of the business cycle they are implemented also matter. For instance, doing trade liberalization—letting imports in and exports out—before financial liberalization—letting people hold any currency they want—yields better growth outcomes. Similarly, more flexible rules for banks to engage in microcredit work better if accompanied by cadastral registries that show who owns what—the two are complementary. In fact, undertaking reforms in several areas at the same time—"in waves"— can significantly amplify gains in productivity, compared with doing them in isolation.[2] The differential impact is not small: the estimated uptick in the five-year average growth in total factor productivity—the best measure of how well a society uses its capital, its workers, and its technology— due to implementing reforms in waves rather than piece- meal is 2 percentage points among advanced and emerging countries, and more than 5 percentage points in low-income ones. And timing can make a difference too: opening an industry to private investors at the bottom of the business cycle—that is, when the economy is in real trouble—does more to boost economic activity than at the peak.

Third, cost is a key factor in choosing reforms—many of them don't come cheap. Lack of resources makes it less attractive for governments to launch reforms whose nega- tive short-term effects call for compensatory expenditures (e.g., helping workers who are laid off because of changes in the labor laws), and it may favor reforms with no imme- diate fiscal cost (e.g., allowing new firms to enter a market).

You may be thinking: Structural reforms sound painful, will they work? Although earlier research showed mixed results, recent empirical evidence has been uniformly positive.[3] Studies have found that reforms in trade and finance significantly raise growth—when you let people buy and sell across borders, and make banks sounder and more accessible, your economy becomes more efficient and more attractive to foreign capital. There is also a positive correlation between faster economic expansion and legal and institutional reforms, particularly in the area of property rights. The less red tape, the better. Breaking up monopolies and letting in new producers boosts total factor productivity. Other types of reform have been shown to carry potentially negative effects on growth in the short term, but positive ones in the long run—that is the case with, for example, changes in some of the rules that govern the labor market and the pension system.

The bottom line is this: structural reform is not easy or popular, but it works. And it may be the only way out when the economy is in a jam.

What is the G20 and why does it matter for development?

The G20 is the gathering forum for the governments of the world's twenty largest economies. It includes economic powerhouses like China, the European Union, and the United States, and up-and-coming emerging markets like India, Indonesia, and Mexico. It started in 1999 as a regular meeting for ministers of finance and central bankers to debate trends and ideas. But the global crisis of 2008–2009 raised its profile and its relevance, and it quickly became a platform for political leaders to coordinate economic policy.

Things have since evolved—a lot. The forum is now anchored around a yearly Leaders' Summit, where presidents, prime ministers, and heads of international organizations make policy commitments and, in principle, hold each other accountable. In between summits, there is a massive amount of representational and technical work. That work is managed along two "tracks"—the "sherpas" (mostly ministers representing their presidents and prime ministers) and the "finance deputies" (who stand in for the finance ministers and central bank governors). Each track meets about five times a year and has formed its own "study" and "working" groups which, in turn, meet as needed. At last count, there were seven groups under the sherpas (anti-corruption, climate finance, development, employment, energy sustainability, growth, and trade and investment) and seven under the finance deputies (anti-terrorist financing, financial sector reform, framework for growth, green finance, international financial architecture, international taxation, and investment and infrastructure). In parallel, there is a G20-sponsored Global Partnership on Financial Inclusion and a series of G20 "ministerial" meetings in sectors such as agriculture, energy, trade, and tourism; each of them builds its own work program.

Unbelievable as it may sound, there are no headquarters, staff, or secretariat. Countries take yearly turns chairing the G20, hosting the summit, and deciding its theme. For example, in 2016, China was the chair, and the theme of the agenda for the year was "An Innovative, Invigorated, Interconnected, and Inclusive World Economy." But, if there is no staff, who does the technical work? This is done by a long list of international organizations—among them, the United Nations, IMF, World Bank, OECD, World Trade Organization, International Labor Organization, and Financial Stability Board. They are commissioned to produce tons of reports, papers, presentations, and commentary.

Why is all this summitry relevant for economic development? Three reasons: size, coordination, and advocacy. The G20 represents about 90 percent of the world's GDP, 80 percent of its trade, and two-thirds of its population. The performance and the policies of these countries define the economic context in which the rest of the world operates. If the G20 sneezes, the non-G20 catches a cold. So any opportunity to improve coordination and reinforce common sense is welcome. Also, the public officials who attend these meetings are the same ones who make decisions on foreign aid, trade preferences, regulation of financial flows, visas for migrants, and many of the issues that matter for developing countries. If there is a place where good ideas can have an impact, it is the G20 gatherings.

As you can imagine, the G20 has at times failed to agree or act—you can't really blame it, as the economic, social, political, and fiscal realities of the member countries do not move in tandem. Each member has its own problems and priorities to deal with. But, to their credit, common positions reached during G20 meetings are the reason why the 2008–2009 crisis did not get much worse, why the global trading system remains open, and why meaningful commitments have been made to stop climate change.

How do governments regulate the financial sector?

The 2008–2009 global crisis, and its many, long-lingering effects, opened the door to new thinking on how to regulate the world of finance—and closed it on some of the previous orthodoxy. There is now broad agreement that lax prudential oversight was the main cause (albeit not the only cause) of the crisis. Financiers were allowed to sell instruments— like "mortgage-backed securities" and "credit default swaps"—that created massive "systemic risk," that is, risk that the failure of one financier could bring down the whole financial system. Many of those transactions were not even recorded on the books of those who took part in them. This has sparked a flurry of reform proposals.

Some of those proposals are focused on the relationship across financial agents—on how one agent's fate is correlated with others'. The core idea is for the government to "tax" (literally or through various forms of capital requirements) banks, hedge funds, and others who can jeopardize the system, not just because they are "too big to fail" but also because they are also "too interconnected to fail." The assumption is that regulation will now reach all agents—the "regulatory perimeter" will expand. In practice, regulators may not have enough information to impose that "tax." So, various proxies for an institution's contribution to systemic risk have been put forward by experts inside and outside governments: sheer size of its balance sheet, degree of leverage, maturity mismatches, and so on. All of them are yet to be tested by experience.

Other financial reform proposals emphasize time—that is, how financial risk changes when the economy grows or contracts. When the economy booms, there is less perceived risk, asset prices rise, and it is easier to borrow. When the economy turns, the opposite happens, perhaps more abruptly. What kind of "macroprudential" regulations can automatically moderate lending in the upswing and ease it during downturns? Two candidates stand out: asking banks, in good times, to put aside more capital or to make larger loan provisions (these, not surprisingly, are called "pro-cyclical capital requirements" and "pro-cyclical loan provisions"). Only the latter has actually been deployed (by Spain, Colombia, and Peru, among others). But the jury is still out on its impact.

Whether reforms in the financial industry are geared toward controlling size, interconnectedness, or timing, there is another potential reason to render their result uncertain at best: lack of international coordination. If countries (developed and developing) adopt different regulatory standards, money—and, with it, risk and bubbles—will fly to the jurisdictions that are less strict or less capable of enforcement. That is thus far the fate of Basel III, the prescribed prudential guidelines sponsored by richer countries, which very few emerging ones have adopted.

Partly to prevent that kind of "regulatory shopping," controls on the movement of capital across borders have become an acceptable tool. They used to be viewed as heretical because they frightened away investors. The difference is that now many of those controls are set up to keep money from flying in rather than flying out. The idea is that "hot money"—cash sent to a country for a very short time to profit from an unusual return—is volatile, can be pulled out at any time, and complicates life for local regulators who prefer stability and predictability.

By now, you may have the feeling that regulatory wisdom is under reconstruction in the financial sector and that it may take years to complete. It is, and it will. That would not be a problem if it were not for the fact that the largest central banks (those in the United States, Europe, England, Japan) have been trying to energize the world's economy by pumping money into it. They now see a bit of inflation (perhaps as high as 4 percent per year) as a good thing, when it was a no-no before. The purpose of this is to avoid a "liquidity trap": when the economy falls into recession, people expect prices to fall, so they delay consumption to buy cheaper later, which makes the recession even worse, then people postpone even more purchases, and so on. Japan has suffered from this problem for years. The downside is that putting a lot of cash in the hands of financiers pushes them to take risks with it. This is how the 2008–2009 crisis started.[4]

Do the Fed's decisions matter to the developing world?

Between 2009 and 2016, the US Federal Reserve—America's central bank—practiced an extraordinary form of monetary policy. The Fed committed to fighting recession by keeping interest rates in the United States close to zero—which meant printing lots of money. That pushed Wall Street bankers to look abroad for higher returns, and it explains most of the surge in gross capital flows toward emerging and developing economies. As a proportion of the recipients' GDP, those flows grew by about half after the global financial crisis of 2008. But as the flows rose, they also became more volatile. Mutual, pension, and insurance funds began to replace banks as the main cross-border investors, while purchases of bonds grew four times faster than those of equity. These kinds of portfolios have proven more sensitive to bad news—whether global or local.

Will those edgy portfolio investors stampede indiscriminately out of—and wreak havoc among—middle- and low-income countries when the Fed finally and significantly lifts interest rates, something its Open Market Committee ponders more than eight times a year? Or will they differentiate and stay in well-managed economies with strong "fundamentals"? With one proviso, you should bet on differentiation. The proviso is this: that higher US interest rates do not trigger financial turmoil in Wall Street.

It is true that for the average developing country macroeconomic fundamentals have been getting worse—not better—since about 2010. Its external position has weakened—the deficit in its balance of payments' current account, a measure of how much a country dissaves, deepened. So has its fiscal position—the deficit in its government's accounts more than doubled. Its debt burden has grown heavier—it is now equivalent to about half its GDP.

It has fewer foreign currency reserves. And it lives in a world economy that is growing more slowly.

But that average country does not actually exist. Investors know that. When global markets were spooked by Greece in 2010 and by talk of "tapering" of US monetary policy in mid-2013 and, again in early 2014, the sell-off of assets from emerging and developing economies happened initially across the board, but soon enough reason prevailed and good performers were spared. This taught us a lesson: what causes indiscriminate withdrawals from emerging and developing markets is global financial *volatility*, not small and predictable changes in interest rates. In a 2015 paper, Swati Ghosh and her colleagues at the World Bank gathered sufficient data to assess the role that volatility plays in bond issuances by emerging and developing countries—the negative impact is huge. This may also explain why policymakers in those countries called for the Fed to *raise* its interest rates—get it done and over with, so the uncertainty ebbs.[5]

This brings us to our proviso. If the Fed's decision to increase interest rates—whenever it comes to that—unveils systemic risk in the US financial markets and, thus, hikes global volatility, the exodus of portfolio investors from the developing world could be large, indiscriminate, and painful. Solid fundamentals would not be much of a protection. How should a developing-country government prepare for such a sudden outflow of capital? We'll talk about that later, but keep in mind five steps: securing financing, prioritizing investments, targeting social expenditures, testing banks, and identifying winners and losers. Of course, it may be too late to do any of this once money starts rushing out, and much of it should be done whatever the Fed decides. But it may help next time around.

What do Europe's woes mean for the world's poor?

Europe's lingering economic troubles—stagnation, unemployment, and aging—have been at the center of global attention for almost a decade. They have been made worse by more recent developments, like Brexit and the rise of nationalism. Can the European Central Bank print enough money to jump-start the continent's economy? Or should that be done through a blast of public investment financed with yet more accumulation of debt? How should Greece be helped? What does the sudden appreciation of the Swiss franc mean for the Eurozone? Will Russia's financial distress spill over to its neighbors? How those questions are answered will affect some of the world's richest countries—the likes of France, Germany, and Italy. What is usually ignored is that they will also affect some of the poorest.

Take the thirty-four economies currently classified by the World Bank as "low-income countries"—LICs in development parlance. They are home to 850 million people whose combined GDP is smaller than that of Switzerland (population 8 million). About half of these people live in a state of extreme poverty, with less than $1.90 a day. What happens to them may not matter economically to Europe; but what happens in Europe matters a great deal to them.

The LICs' exposure to Europe comes through four channels—trade, remittances, aid, and finance. A third of Bangladesh's and Mozambique's exports, and half of Madagascar's, go to Europe. The average LIC sells almost as much to Europe as it does to China—its largest customer. But China itself is slowing down, after a binge of infrastructure construction that left its provinces and counties three trillion dollars in debt: a lesson that policymakers in Brussels should heed as they look for ways to restart growth.

Each year, migrants from some of the smallest LICs work in Europe and send money home. The amounts may sound insignificant in London or Paris, but they are huge for Gambia and Togo—around 3 percent of their GDP, roughly equivalent to what their governments spend on healthcare. Research has shown that remittances are surprisingly resilient to the vagaries of the host economies—migrants prefer to tighten their own belts rather than cut transfers to their families.[6] But, after so many years of stagnation, how long before the flow of remittances from Europe to the LICs begins to dry up?

What shouldn't dry up is foreign aid. Since the global financial crisis erupted in 2008–2009, the members of the European Union have not drastically cut their aid budgets as a percent of their GDP, even when they have been forced by the recession to cut public services to their own citizens. They deserve praise for that. The problem is that as their GDP shrinks, the value of their donations shrinks too. This can hurt countries like Liberia, where European aid covers more than half of all public expenditures.

And then there is finance. As the Euro loses value, many LICs have had to recalibrate their borrowing strategies. Think of the fourteen west and central African countries whose common currency—the CFA franc—is pegged to the Euro. As their currency depreciates, their exports become more competitive. But their debts, which are almost entirely denominated in US dollars, become more difficult to service. Fortunately, over the past decade or so, the public debts of many LICs were forgiven—by, among others, European governments. Still, a typical LIC carries today a stock of public external debt worth a quarter of its GDP—not trivial when you have children in need of food, education, or vaccinations. Data on private financing for LICs is sketchier, but we know that European firms implement four of every ten new investment projects in Africa, a proportion that has not changed much for a while. One hopes they can keep their nerves.

Overall, the LICs' exposure to Europe is major but, so far, manageable. This, of course, assumes that the European Union remains a functioning single market with a common currency. The alternative—with one or more members facing sovereign debt defaults, bans on capital outflows, controls on imports, and bursts of xenophobia—would spread uncertainty and pain well beyond its borders. The world's poorest nations have an interest in a united, stable, and prosperous Europe.

How do you prepare for the next global crisis?

Imagine you are minister of finance in an average developing country. You survived the 2008–2009 global crisis and presided over more than six years of respectable economic growth. A boom in commodity prices fills your treasury with cash, international bankers queue outside your office to offer you loans, and your central bank does not quite know how to keep your currency from *appreciating*. Old problems persist—too many young people are unemployed, your industrial sector is small and aging, and plenty of public money is wasted or simply missing. But, all in all, you feel pretty good about how things are going under your watch.

Suddenly you learn that a new global crisis may be looming on the horizon. Think of a rich country defaulting on its debt or closing its economy, pulling other rich countries' banks into trouble. East Asia can no longer find avid consumers in the West for its exports, so it cuts back its own consumption of raw materials. Commodity prices begin to fall, and your politicians start to worry aloud. What do you do then? Or better, what can you do *now* to prepare for all that? Five key measures may help.

First, secure your financing—for at least the next twenty-four months. The last thing you want in the middle of a storm in international finance is to default on your payments. If you do, already nervous investors—foreign and local—will rush for your economy's door. We could also speak of what soldiers, teachers, and civil servants would do if they were to go unpaid. So, calculate your cash needs as if all your expenditures were untouchable, and sign today the loans you know you will need tomorrow. While you are at it, assume that a good 10 percent of those grants that developed nations regularly give you will no longer come in—after all, those nations will be entangled in austerity, absorbed by their own problems. It would be nice as well if the public companies that manage your oil, gas, or minerals could buy insurance against their prices falling too much (this is called "hedging" in financial jargon); unfortunately, if they have not done it before, it is probably too late now—the legal and administrative arrangements are not easy.

Second, prioritize your investments. Decide now which projects you will slow down, postpone, or drop if you were to run out of money. In a way, you are looking for projects that are not "shovel ready," that is, those that cannot be quickly implemented. Rule of thumb: if it involves massive, never-done-before, pride-of-the-nation construction, it probably can be put on hold. Remember that cutting investment expenditures is always tricky—the interests of the politically connected are usually affected. You don't want to have that discussion during a crisis.

Third, audit your social safety nets. There will be plenty of people in need as jobs disappear and incomes fall. Poor families will respond in ways that may hurt them and your country in the long run—pulling teenagers out of high school is the typical example. You will then be called upon to fund temporary employment programs, feed children in schools, and pay for direct cash transfers. If you don't have the necessary logistics in place—including an updated register of who is poor and how to reach them—you better start working on it. There will be no time for this when the turmoil begins.

Fourth, "stress-test" your banks. Your financial system is probably small and isolated from the subprime sophistication of Wall Street. It is most likely made up of banks that hold the deposits of the urban middle class and handle the remittances of the diaspora. What would happen to your banks if, all of a sudden, foreign currency became expensive and scarce? Are their loans concentrated on a few construction or trading companies that would go belly up if the commodity boom came to an end? And are banks lending to each other? To each other's owners? Your central bank should be able to answer all these questions—it is supposed to supervise banks in real time. So it can alert you early.

And, fifth, identify who will suffer when crisis strikes. Who are the winners and losers? (Yes, there are winners in this.) Will the impact be felt in a single, remote rural area where your commodities are produced or extracted, or will it be primarily an industrial affair, hurting middle classes across cities? Will the affected belong to a specific racial, religious, or regional group? Whose consumption will become more expensive? And whose assets will lose most value? This kind of "political economy analysis" is invaluable because it will highlight the roadblocks in your decision-making process.

One final step may not depend entirely on the finance minister. This step is to decide who, when the time comes, will speak for the government and what the message will be. Typically, in days of turbulence, cabinets tend to become dissonant and perceptions of policy paralysis—if not incompetence—make things worse. That would be a pity. All told, it is possible—and not too difficult—to get ready, at least for the first wave of impacts from a potential new global crisis. Yet if the crisis never comes, so much the better.

Was the commodity bonanza wasted?

Until mid-2014, commodity prices had been sky-high for almost a decade. They were then brought down by a combination of disagreement among oil producers, a stagnant world economy, and lower relative demand by a burgeoning global middle class. At the same time, new exploration technologies boosted the rate of discovery—you've probably heard of "fracking" and how it has broken open formerly inaccessible gas deposits. Was this commodity bonanza wasted, especially in developing countries whose exports and fiscal revenues depend on natural resources? Not quite. But don't uncork the champagne just yet.

The literature on whether commodity wealth is a curse or a blessing is as vast as it is ambivalent. What is certain from empirical evidence is that good policies and good governance are necessary, but not sufficient, conditions for natural riches (especially oil and minerals) to support development. For that to happen, it is necessary to solve five main problems associated with those riches: (1) something called the "Dutch Disease" (noncommodity exports becoming less competitive), (2) price volatility (complicating investment decisions), (3) overborrowing (lenders are less stringent with governments that expect to collect lots of cash), (4) sustainability (the amount of natural wealth to preserve for future generations), and (5) corruption (the larger the rent, the more voracious the graft).

Given these five challenges, has the developing world succeeded where it had mostly failed before? It has not yet succeeded, but this time around, it has done better. With important differences across countries, democratization has, on average, enhanced citizens' demand for transparency and has improved institutional checks and balances. In parallel, natural resource funds have become more common and the technology to administer them has improved. Public investment processes, from identification to evaluation, are also better.

More generally, fiscal policy is more robust, backed by more rules, better coordinated with other agencies of the state (notably, central banks), and more acquainted with techniques for results-based management. Monetary policy is stronger too (scores of countries follow and meet inflation targets, with little or no political meddling). And while we are still far away from a broad acceptance of the prudent "permanent income rule" (that is, from spending only a conservatively estimated return from our natural wealth), there is a general sense among policymakers and voters that consumption binges financed by commodity revenues tend to end in tears.

Of course, not all developing countries have improved their natural resource management at the same speed, and a few have actually moved in the opposite direction. But the overall trend is more promising than it has ever been. The more the rich nations undergo painful fiscal adjustments and austerity, the more support politicians in emerging markets will have for prudence in saving and using commodity wealth. It may sound overly optimistic, but sensible fiscal management will begin to be perceived as a political asset.[7]

Will globalization end?

Over the past three decades, global trade grew almost twice as fast as the global economy. The massive process of commercial integration was made possible by technological revolutions in transport (like containerized shipping) and communications technologies, and by a dramatic decline in import tariffs. This allowed many developing countries to implement export-led growth strategies that lifted hundreds of millions of people out of poverty. Some succeeded in sought-after manufacture markets and, more recently, even in services.

But the 2008–2009 global financial crisis showed the volatile side of integration. In two years, the volume of world trade fell by one-third and international production networks carried along country-to-country contagion at staggering speed. By 2016, that volume was not growing at all. More dangerously, Brexit happened, and radical politicians the world over began to voice discontent with the free trade agreements that underpin globalization—they represent the feelings of those whose livelihoods were lost to foreign competition or who are threatened by it.

Will the world throw the baby out with the bath water and revert to economic isolation? The probability of going back to preglobalization, import-substituting industrial policy is not high, but it is not negligible either—concern for unemployment may still trigger protectionism, especially among rich nations. More likely, public policy will, in most countries, take an "enlightened path" that uses the power of the state to make markets work better. Over the next decade, that path—call it "export-led growth 2.0" if you want—will still involve the traditional prescriptions of sound macroeconomic fundamentals, qualified human capital, and efficient institutions. It will also involve renewed efforts at the less glamorous art of facilitating trade—things like reducing the cost of moving goods (more competition in logistics markets, faster border agencies), helping exporters survive (stable finance, maintenance of standards, certifications, and licenses), linking export-processing zones with local clusters (more flexible zone rules), and enhancing the practical value of export promotion (dissemination of best practices and commercial intelligence).

But, strategically, the "enlightened path" will be defined by three new, powerful trends in global trade. First, South–South integration. With the United States, the Eurozone, and Japan forced to "rebalance" their saving-consumption mix in favor of the former, commerce among developing countries will play a much larger role. More advanced emerging markets will account for a larger share of the demand for LICs' exports. A multipolar pattern of global growth will emerge. In fact, the 2008–2009 crisis only accelerated a decline in the relative importance of rich-country demand that had started almost two decades before. This does not mean that South–South trade will be easy. Consumers in developing countries care more about price than quality or variety. Import tariffs are higher, by several multiples, compared with the OECD countries, and investment climates are worse.

Second, the new trade strategies will put a higher premium on diversification, not only of partners but also of products, as an insurance against volatility. Expect more sophisticated trade agreements, and more mutual surveillance among developing countries. And expect innovation to be the new code word for trade success. The quest for new brands and niches will dominate the second generation of internal reforms—from research and development incentives to tertiary education curricula.

And third, social concerns will play a much bigger role in trade agreements. Those concerns were there previously, but not much was actually done about them. People who lost their jobs because they could not compete internationally rarely got the income support, skill retraining, and market information that they needed to start over in a different industry—no wonder they distrust anything coming from abroad, from multinationals to immigrants. They will force future trade negotiations to be more transparent and more inclusive. This will slow down progress, but it will make the outcome more sustainable.

Will exchange-rate manipulation be an effective, even common, instrument in the new multipolar, diversification-driven, socially conscious trade framework? Unlikely. The proliferation of production chains, where import content is critical for exports, would not sit well with artificially high exchange rates. For most countries, the cost of managed undervaluation in terms of reserve accumulation and inflationary pressures would prove unbearable (to keep foreign currency dear, your central bank needs to buy a lot of it, for which it has to print a lot of your country's own currency). And the uncertainty associated with large exchange-rate misalignments would hinder export-oriented investments.

In sum, the crisis and its long economic and political aftermath will not usher in the end of globalization. But it will bring about a new kind of globalization. This time, it will take place mostly in the developing world, will be led by those countries that have more ideas—not necessarily more resources—and will be more socially sustainable.[8]

Why does growth happen in some places and not in others?

Have you ever wondered why, sometimes, poverty seems entrenched in countries that otherwise grow fast? Take the case of India, a model of economic takeoff. Its extreme poverty rate—that is, the proportion of its population living on $1.90 a day or less—has fallen by more than half since the 1990s. Today, it stands at about 12 percent, affecting 170 million Indians. But falling rates don't mean much to you if you happen to be among those 170 million, that is, those who don't have enough to eat. What explains these masses of poverty inside otherwise successful economies?

A book edited by Ejaz Ghani of the World Bank looks at South Asia—the part of the world with the largest concentration of poor people—and concludes that the main culprit is, believe it or not, geography.[9]

Economic activity tends to concentrate—to "agglomerate" in technical speak. Producers want to be close to consumers. This allows them to cut transportation costs. It also helps them acquire information, especially on tastes and technologies. More important, proximity allows them to take advantage of "economies of scale"—you can produce cheaper TV sets if you make a million of them instead of a thousand. Why? Because the cost of your initial investment can be divided among a larger number of customers. (NB: the initial investment could be money you spent on a plant or on researching and developing an idea.) So firms tend to locate where the market is, workers follow firms, the market gets bigger, more firms move closer to the market, more workers follow those new firms, and on it goes. You have a virtuous circle of development. Of course, the "market" can be just a large city or a city with a port from which you can ship things abroad—from where you can go global. Just think why New York, London, Mumbai, or Shanghai became what they are.

The problem comes when, for some reason, people do not follow jobs—when they do not migrate, or not in sufficient numbers, which seems to be the case in South Asia. Then, a country gets split into "leading" and "lagging" regions. The former become more productive, more globalized, and more technologically sophisticated. The latter get stuck at low levels of income, mostly relying on subsistence agriculture. In the aggregate and from the outside, the country may look very good (who would question India's shining future?), but a mass of poverty remains at its core. True, when the economy as a whole grows fast, everyone may benefit, even if indirectly—after all, the income of poor farmers depends on selling their produce to rich urbanites. But what almost never happens is that lagging regions catch up. There is no convergence—if anything, there is divergence. You may think: So what if a few provinces remain backwaters, as long as the nation progresses? Well, experience suggests that regional disparity breeds violent conflict, and eventually everybody is worse off—pick any recent civil war and chances are that it is rooted in grossly uneven development.

What should governments do and not do? The first obvious tool is a progressive system that shares the taxes collected by the central government among regions—that is, transfer more money to poorer provinces and municipalities. In a way, richer regions subsidize poorer ones. In practice, this rarely solves the problem. Governors and mayors in lagging areas usually lack the capacity to invest the money well or to use it to improve public services critical for development, like education and health. Things get even more complicated if the transfers are paid for with sales of oil, gas, or minerals extracted from the less developed parts of a country, whose residents may then feel that they do not profit enough from their own resources. You will find many cases of this in West Africa.

Second, governments should help people migrate. This is less dramatic than it sounds. When the workers of a lagging region leave for better jobs elsewhere, they send remittances home, and wages improve for those left behind. Over time, everyone is better off. China is a good example of this. The problem is that, many times, governments get in the way. By granting subsidies to specific activities in specific places—say, giving away fertilizers for rice cultivation in faraway villages where water is scarce—they force people to stay put, producing something they may not be competitive at, lest they lose the subsidy. On the other hand, the kind of public investment that would help mobility—like portable skills and employment services—often is missing in lagging areas. Ergo, people get geographically "trapped" in poverty.

And, third, governments should make it easier for agriculture to become "commercialized," that is, for larger enterprises to start working the land with the kind of equipment, technology, and management that can make local produce exportable. This, in effect, connects lagging regions with the rest of the world. It could take the form of small farmers forming cooperatives. More likely, it means reform in land ownership—giving rural families clear titles to their plots, which allow them to sell if they want and migrate if they wish. This was one of the keys to Brazil's success in transforming its "Cerrado"—a giant savannah that was once known for its remote backwardness—into a global agricultural player.

What if transfers from the central government, migration, and agricultural transformation do not work? Are lagging regions condemned? Not necessarily. Technology may still change the geography of economic growth. The Web has brought people together, wherever they live. It has also made information more accessible to firms, wherever they locate. Cheaper transportation has fomented the breakup of the production chain—the final product is assembled with parts made in many locations, usually across country borders, allowing less developed regions to contribute the easier components. East Asia is a pioneer of this. Most promising, new production techniques—keep an eye on "three-dimensional printing" and driverless cars—have reduced the importance of "economies of scale."[10] One day, size will no longer matter. (Auto industry experts say that Detroit's car manufacturers can now break even in new models if they sell about two hundred thousand units, instead of over one million as in the past.)

So, the overall point is clear: with time, regional disparities may very well disappear by themselves. But for countries that cannot wait—and for political reasons most cannot—government action is not only possible but also necessary.

Why is it so difficult to agree on tax reform?

We see it today in the United States. We saw it in India in 2010, in Mexico in 2007, and almost everywhere else in the past two decades. Around the world, comprehensive tax reform has been difficult—if not impossible. Rich or poor, countries have rarely managed to clean up their tax "codes"—the thousands of pages through which sales, income, property, value-added, inheritance, and many other taxes are imposed on all of us. At most, governments have added patches to what was already a patchwork of previous attempts at reform. Why? Don't we need taxes to pay for public schools, hospitals, and roads? Can't we just agree on a system that is simple, fair, and sufficient? Well, it's complicated. When you design a tax system, you are trying to hit six—sometimes contradictory—objectives at the same time.

First, you want every tax to actually raise significant revenue. Why go through the administrative and political pain of having a tax if the money collected will be puny? Yes, you can put a tax on twelve-year-old whiskies or on twelve-cylinder luxury cars. But how good is it if so few people consume those goods that, at the end of the day, the revenue from the tax is spent chasing cheaters? You want taxes to be "broad-based," that is, to cover a wide range of consumptions or incomes. (By the way, a good rule of thumb is that the total collection from all taxes together should not be less than one-fifth, and no more than one-third, of the value of the total production in the economy.)

Second, you do not want to alter people's behaviors too much. In technical parlance, you want your tax system to be "efficient," that is, not to push investors, savers, employers, workers, and consumers to do things they would not do if there were no taxes. The typical case is the entrepreneur who opens a factory in the middle of nowhere just to benefit from a tax break that is only given there. But think also of the couple that gets married only because it is "better for tax purposes." Or the lone widow who buys a bigger house just to claim the "mortgage interest break." Seriously, taxes can make you do crazy things.

Third, equity. Notice that it does not say "equality"—it says "equity." You want those that *have* more to *pay* more. But not just dollar for dollar. You want them to pay *proportionally* more. If you earn a hundred thousand dollars, you pay 25 percent. If you earn a million dollars, you pay 40 percent. The tax *rate* goes up with your income. That is called *progressivity* and, of course, it is one of the most contentious aspects of any tax system. The Left loves it; the Right hates it. (More on this later.)

Fourth, administrative simplicity. This is the one condition everyone agrees on—and usually the one we fail to meet. Imagine a flat, 10 percent income tax for everybody on all sources of income—no thresholds, exceptions, deductions, credits, or loopholes of any sort. Such a tax would be very simple to calculate and collect. The corresponding law could fit onto a single page—not to mention the tax return. And being only 10 percent, there would be little incentive to dodge it. But it would probably generate plenty of social tension and resistance. Why are the ultra-poor paying the same rate as the ultra-rich? Why do you get the same deductions—that is, none—whether you have one child or five? In other words, simplicity and equity can clash.

Fifth, federal consistency. At any point in time, there are several governments trying to tax you. In addition to the federal taxman, you need to consider taxes paid to your state, your county, and even your city. The last thing you want is for them to all tax you for the same thing—"double" or "triple" taxation. So the various levels of government have learned to share "tax bases" according to their respective capacity to administer them. For example, it is easier for your municipality to know how much your house is worth and bill you for your property tax—the assessor probably lives close by—than for the federal government, which may be very far away, to do the same thing. But only the federal government can track the income of a corporation that operates in many states, let alone many countries. You get the point.

Finally, tax reform needs to pass through the legislature. Political feasibility is the minimum threshold. Here is where the economists' rubber meets the voters' road. At least in democracies, people's preferences and perceptions matter more than technical beauty. A crystal-clear example: it is technically preferable to apply the VAT to every good and service, without exemptions. This avoids "identification" problems—who says that a bottle of champagne is less "food" than a bottle of milk, or an injection of Botox is less "medicine" than an injection of antibiotics? But most politicians, especially in developing countries, would think twice before allowing food and medicine to be subject to VAT. They say it would hurt the poor. They are right: food accounts for a higher portion of a poor family's budget. The theoretical solution is to compensate those in poverty through direct social assistance (read: cash transfers) and let the VAT be as "universal" as possible. In practice, food and medicine remain untaxed in many—if not most—countries.

So there you have it: revenue generation, economic efficiency, social equity, administrative simplicity, federal consistency, and political feasibility—all need to be achieved at the same time. Is it possible? Yes, but it needs a lot of public education and communication to explain why everyone has to be inside the tax net and why some have to carry a heavier burden than others. It needs a strong civil service that can speak truth to political power without fear. And, most importantly, it needs politicians who are not polarized, and who can negotiate trade-offs. But don't blame politicians: they just reflect—or should reflect— the wishes of citizens. The real reason comprehensive tax reforms are so rare is that not many societies have come to agree on a vision of what they want from government— that is, *which* public services should be provided and *who* should pay for them.

What is the global tax war?

Tax avoidance and tax evasion—the former is legal, the latter is not—by multinational corporations and wealthy individuals has for ages been the subject of debate. But, until recently, the debate was mostly among technical experts fighting over arcane concepts like transfer pricing, tax preferences, and double taxation. Enter the Luxemburg-leaks, the Swiss-leaks, the Panama Papers, and the EU-Apple dispute. The public is suddenly outraged over the perception that the powerful are not paying their fair share of taxes. And outraged they should be: the OECD estimates that various sorts of tax havens cost the world somewhere between one hundred billion and a quarter-trillion dollars per year, and that is just in corporate income taxes.[11] Developing countries and their advocates join the fray. They claim that foreign firms shift their profits abroad and pay less taxes than they should for the oil, gas, and minerals that they extract. This has to hurt because, as a proportion of its GDP, an average LIC collects only half the tax revenue that is collected by its rich peers—about 20 percent. Inevitably, politicians react, promising to enforce their national tax rules, whether they clash with those of other countries or not. A "tax war" is afoot.

Will it come to that? Probably not, but when it comes to international coordination, you never know. There are four frontlines in this potential war, and each has its own dynamics. First, multinationals versus tax administrators. There is evidence corporations that operate globally shift profits from high- to low-tax jurisdictions. This, which is not always illegal, is particularly difficult to catch when a company's main assets are intangible— like patents or brands. It is usually driven by countries offering tax breaks to attract investment; they compel other countries to offer ever bigger breaks. The proper answer to this tax competition is not crackdowns; it is more harmonization and better sharing of information. Some of that is happening, so far mostly among OECD members.

Second, OECD countries versus other OECD countries. The headline cases have to do with quirks in the US tax code. It allows American companies to hold profits abroad free of tax and, until recently, to relocate their headquarters overseas for tax purposes—something strangely called "corporate inversion." This spreads conflict with tax agencies outside the United States. Apple's and Google's troubles in Europe, and Burger King's in Canada, are related to that. Until now, each claim has been dealt with individually. One would expect a broader solution through comprehensive tax reform in America. That may take years.

Third, developed versus developing countries. Most of these disputes are rooted in bilateral tax treaties that have become outdated, the need to attract investors to poor countries, and the limited capacity of their tax authorities. Picture a government in a poor country eager to attract foreign companies to explore for oil. It grants large tax exemptions and generous royalties. A billion dollar investment in offshore wells is made by a multinational, oil is found, and exports start. Suddenly the price of oil skyrockets and the company makes a fortune, but its tax payments barely change. Political pressure mounts for the national treasury to share in the windfall. A controversy follows, over the concession contract and over the calculation of the taxes due. It is a team of thousand-dollar-an-hour, battle-tested, international lawyers, accountants, and lobbyists against a minister and a few junior staff on local salaries with no experience. Who do you think carries the day? In no time, the matter becomes a bilateral confrontation between the two countries involved—and a source of lasting resentment.

And fourth, it is wealthy elites versus regular taxpayers. The former have the information and the means to exploit every tax loophole there is wherever it is—nothing necessarily illegal about that. The latter just pay their taxes and feel cheated by an inequitable system. Progressivity—that is, when your effective tax *rate* increases with your income—goes out the window. So, with every new media disclosure of abuse by the 1 percent, public demands for action multiply. Politicians promise to end the injustice once and for all. But nothing much really happens.

Because of inaction or because of lack of international coordination, those four frontlines are worrisome. But there is a sliver of restraint running through them. The probability of a global tax war breaking out will be curbed by a very practical consideration: in an interconnected world, smart governments do not want to scare away investors. Both corporations and individuals can leave or stay away from a location where taxes are unpredictable—they tend to "de-risk" their investment plans. In this war, expect a lot of posturing but little actual fighting.

3

SOCIAL POLICY

OLD WAR, NEW WEAPONS

Why did Piketty's work pique our sudden interest in inequality?

The publication in 2014 of Thomas Piketty's *Capital in the Twenty-First Century* brought inequality to the center of the public policy debate.[1] Looking at lots of historical data, Piketty found that the return on capital is always higher than economic growth. That means that those who own capital will do better than the rest. The rich will not just get richer, but they will also get richer than everyone else. In capitalism, if governments do nothing, wealth is bound to concentrate among the few.

This argument has attracted many followers. Joseph Stiglitz, a Nobel laureate, published in 2015 *The Great Divide*, a kind of application of Piketty to the United States.[2] (Disclaimer: When Stiglitz presented his book in Washington in the spring of 2015, I chaired the event.) But there are also many would-be debunkers—one of them has shown that wealth does not concentrate as much if you take housing out of the data.[3]

For most economists, all this is puzzling—the study of inequality has been going on for a long time. To give you an idea, the index used to measure how unequal the distribution of income is—the "Gini coefficient"—was invented a century ago. Why the sudden interest? Why worry now about something that has been the fodder of academics, politicians, and the media for so long? Here are four likely reasons.

First, we still don't know how much inequality we should live with. While most people detest extreme inequality, most people also detest extreme equality. No one likes to hear that the world's richest 1 percent will soon be wealthier than the rest of us put together.[4] But no one really wants to see governments forcing us to own or earn the same whatever our efforts or talents are. How equal should societies be? Economics provides only part of the answer.

Research shows that countries where inequality is rampant tend to grow more slowly in the long run and to recover more slowly after a recession.[5,6] And we suspect that there is a direct link between large income differences and political instability, civil conflict, populism, and criminality—none of which is costless. But economists cannot settle what is, in essence, a matter of social choice. At least in democracies, voters can choose how much inequality they are willing to tolerate by picking a leader that represents their views. The problem, as Stiglitz will rightly tell you, is that inequality can ruin democracy itself: the rich elite just captures the politicians. Ergo: Social policy rarely reflects social preferences.

Second, we may be worrying about the wrong problem. The current debate is about inequality of *outcomes among adults*, that is, how much wealth, income, land, or education each of them should get. In that, there is no agreement. But there is agreement about inequality of *opportunity among children*—there should be none. A child's success in life should not depend on her birthplace, gender, race, family's worth, or any other personal circumstance over which she has no control or responsibility. This is held true across the political spectrum—for the Left as a matter of social justice, and for the Right as a matter of individual merit. Unfortunately, it was not until 2008 that the first Human Opportunity Index was constructed and published, and applied to Latin America—a region where inequality is rife.[7] Few countries currently use it to guide social policy and public expenditures (Colombia has been a leader in this). That will change over time.

Third, we are focusing on radical rather than practical solutions. Piketty suggests a global tax on capital—wherever your wealth sits, it would be taxed at the same rate. This is a good idea in theory. But if taxes are difficult to agree on inside a single country, how likely is an agreement among the 196 countries of the world? Stiglitz and others propose free public services *for all*—things like healthcare, college education, and transportation. Taken literally, this would make inequality worse because it would take money from programs that could benefit the poor—imagine spending scarce public dollars on paying for rich kids to get a university degree. In fact, the opposite may be better—governments should focus more of their spending on those in need and away from the well-off.

Take fuel subsidies. In the average developing country, *two-thirds* of gasoline subsidies go to the rich, as they have the cars. Only 3 percent goes to the poor, as they rely on public transportation, where it exists. Something similar happens with electricity and natural gas—who owns the larger houses? This is a fiscal aberration that can be corrected. The technology to identify and transfer money to the poor—and only to the poor—exists and is cheap. What is lacking is political will.

Finally, we may be perpetuating inequality with our own behaviors. There is growing evidence that, in increasing numbers, people marry people like themselves.[8]

This "sorting" is based mostly on education—think of Ivy leaguers marrying only other Ivy leaguers, and high school dropouts marrying only high school dropouts. The educated choose the educated, and so do their kids. Contacts, jobs, and assets then get trapped into classes. Serious scholars have found that if marriages had occurred at random across educational levels, the distribution of household income in the United States today would not be much different from what it was in the 1960s, that is, before the "Great Divide" opened up.[9]

For now, most of the research comes from developed countries, but the findings probably resonate if you live in Africa, South Asia, or Latin America. Can governments change our social attitudes? Not easily. Perhaps our newly found obsession with inequality is a reflection of a collective sense of guilt.

How many people live in extreme poverty?

Every year, for the past thirty-five years, the World Bank has published the World Development Indicators (WDI), a fine collection of data on developing countries. The 2016 issue of the WDI is unusually telling.[10] Deep into the report, there is a table that shows the status and the evolution of extreme poverty, that is, of people who live on $1.90 a day or less.[11] Think about it: $1.90 a day. How would your life look if you had to live on that? To start with, your house— if you had something that could be called a house—would have no electricity, gas, running water, or sewer. So no TV, refrigerator, showers, or toilet for you. How about toothpaste, contraceptives, or motorized transportation? You'd surely not spend your $1.90 on any of that. If you got sick—which would be very likely in your sanitary and nutritional condition—you would not be able to afford any medicine. In fact, you'd save your meager cash to buy food, just to keep yourself and your family alive. It would add up to a miserable existence, wouldn't it? It is even difficult to imagine that, in the twenty-first century, anyone lives such a nineteenth-century life.

Well, some eight hundred million people do, according to the 2016 WDI. (NB: measuring global poverty is no technical picnic, as prices, exchange rates, methods, definitions, and frequencies vary across countries and across time.) That's a huge proportion of the world's seven billion human beings. It makes you wonder what development experts and financiers have been doing all these years. And yet, behind the horror, shame, and urgency of those figures, there is, believe it or not, hope.

First, one region proved that fast economic growth can squash extreme poverty. In the twenty years through 2012, the proportion of people living on $1.90 a day or less in East Asia fell from over half of the population to less than one-tenth. That's about 850 million people lifted up from indigence. History has never seen anything like it. And the forecast is that in the next five years, even that tenth will be cut in half. Yes, most of it is due to one country—China. Still, it proves to the rest of the world that it can be done.

Second, the global financial crisis of 2008–2009 did not increase extreme poverty—if anything, it only slowed temporarily the downward trend that extreme poverty had been on. The fears that contagion from the economic troubles of the rich countries would push even more people toward the very bottom did not materialize. How come? It's not obvious. It may be that when you are so poor, you are almost disconnected from the volatility of formal markets—you live off your tiny plot of land, get few public services, and do not deal with banks.

Third, Africa clocked almost twenty years of continuous decline in extreme poverty—from 61 percent in 1993 to 43 percent in 2012. That's, of course, little consolation for the almost half of all Africans—some four hundred million of them—who haven't yet escaped abject need. And, as other regions have done better, Africa is now home to one-half of the world's extreme poor—up from 15 percent in 1990. For a continent whose economies have been growing apace for a decade, the message is clear: growth is not always enough.

Fourth, progress in the fight against poverty went well beyond money. Ushered by the United Nations, the international community has committed to monitoring seventeen "Sustainable Development Goals" and over 160 "targets," which it promises to reach by 2030. They range from no hunger and good education to gender equality and sustainable cities. The good news is that encouraging results have been recorded for most of them, although with important differences across countries,

Fifth, the future looks good—relatively speaking. The WDI projects that if the world's economy grows over the next fifteen years as fast as it did during the last decade, another five hundred million people will come out of extreme poverty by 2030. The bulk of them will be in East and South Asia. These projections depend on many things going right and assume away further global crises. They also assume no major additional push by governments to end the scandal of people living on $1.90 a day.

This brings us to the final, and perhaps most important, message embedded in the 2016 WDI. When you look at the list of countries with the highest incidence of extreme poverty—say, above 40 percent of the population—you can't help noting that most of them are rich or very rich in natural resources, things like oil, gas, or minerals. How costly would it be for those governments to identify their extreme poor and transfer to them enough cash to raise them out of their misery? As it happens, it would not be costly at all. In this economist's calculation for a sample of African countries, it would cost less than 3 percent of the annual fiscal revenue from the sale of natural resources. How about the logistics of identifying the poor and transferring money to them? Will that be a problem? Nope: biometrics and the Internet have made all that doable and cheap—see India and Mexico. So, why is it not done? Sooner or later, it will be. But that's a different conversation altogether.

How can we help the new poor?

Imagine you were a civil servant. You had four-week vacations, free healthcare, and job security. You looked forward to retiring at fifty-something. And, like the rest of your countrymen, your family enjoyed services that were heavily subsidized—from electricity to transportation to college, you never paid the real cost of what you consumed. Life was good. You were squarely middle class and never really asked who paid for it all.

Suddenly, your government runs out of money and of lenders, and totters toward bankruptcy. In a rush toward austerity, the public sector begins to shed workers and raise prices, and parts of it are sold to private investors who shed even more workers and raise prices even more. You get fired and thrown into a labor market where there are no jobs on offer. Your house is now worth half what you paid for it, and, anyway, you borrowed to buy it. You begin to tap your savings, assuming, of course, that the bank where you have your deposits has not gone bust. You realize that you need to adjust your standard of living—downward, big time. How soon before you fall beneath the "poverty line"? And once you have fallen, who will help you back up? Your broke government? Other countries' governments? Charities? The World Bank? What will they *really* be able to do for you?

You see, helping the ex–middle class or, rather, the "new poor" is not easy. Most social assistance systems are—for good reason—designed to help those who have always been poor, those whom economists call the "structurally poor." The typical social program deals with things like basic health, primary education, and nutrition. That is of little use to educated, middle-aged adults who suddenly lose their income and their assets. The lingering effects of the 2008–2009 global crisis, especially its European victims, have forced us to rethink the objectives and tools of social policy. Past meltdowns in Asia, Eastern Europe, and Latin America provide us with some good hints on what to expect and how to respond.

Start with the fact that the new poor are easier to identify—they have IDs and property titles. They are more likely to live in cities than be dispersed in remote villages. Any help you give them should be easier to target, monitor, and evaluate. The first lifeline is typically unemployment insurance, if it exists. If it doesn't, your best bet is to extend the direct cash or food transfers that you make to the "old poor" and cover their newly minted peers. If you don't have those transfers, then it is down to temporary employment in public works, right? Not quite. It will take a long period of pain before a former middle-classer will accept painting schools or digging water lines. And that assumes that the government can afford to "make work" in the first place.

Second, you don't need to build the human capital of newly poor families—you need to protect it. They will ditch private medical insurance and will show up at public hospitals, but usually when it is too late—they really don't want to go there if they can avoid it. Ditto for private education: public schools' rosters will balloon. The hardest hit may pull their teenagers from high school altogether and send them to work in the informal economy—few of those kids ever return to studying. To make matters worse, the evidence shows that the poorer the country, the more likely students are to drop out. (Interesting: School enrollment increased in the United States during the Great Depression, but nose-dived in almost every African country that went through serious economic malaise.) So you may need to give grants to "at-risk" students just to keep them in class.

Third, those that fall from the middle class during crises usually have solid basic skills. They may need some retraining, but not much. What they don't have is information on where and in which industry the new jobs are—and are not. So anything that you can do to put employers and employees together is doubly valuable. This is the time to invest in government-subsidized employment centers.

Fourth, you should help people get rid of their houses when they can no longer afford them, rather than use public money to refinance their mortgages. Why? Because a house means being stuck in one place where there may or may not be jobs—the huge differences in unemployment levels among American cities are a testament to that. At times of crisis, mobility is crucial.

Finally, don't expect much help from donors—public or private. The reason is simple: there is less sympathy for the fallen middle class. There are no malnourished babies with bloated stomachs in the evening news. No refugee camps. No raging epidemics. These are people who may still dress and look like, well, yourself. They just happened to have lost their livelihood and their lifestyle. It is difficult to convince taxpayers and philanthropists to give more money to United Nations agencies, international development banks, or NGOs to assist poor people who don't (yet) seem poor. And even if they give you the money, those institutions may not have the know-how or the capacity to move quickly enough.

But moving quickly is what they may have to do. Free falls down the social ladder are no academic curiosity. More than one in ten Mexicans fell under the "poverty line" in the year that followed the country's 1994 financial crisis. Fifteen percent of Indonesians suffered the same fate in 1997. So did one in six Russians in 1998. The numbers are even worse for Argentines: one-fifth of them were ejected from the middle class and into poverty during the twelve months that followed their economy's meltdown of 2001. In 2012, one-fourth of all Spaniards were said to be "at risk" of falling into poverty because of the Euro crisis. This kind of social impact is enough to cause major political turmoil and is not easy to turn back. (To give you an idea, it is said that in "normal times" it takes steady, annual economic growth of 5 percent or more to reduce poverty by 1 percentage point each year.) The longer a crisis lingers, the more urgent it is to line up the tools, the policies, and the institutions that will deal with the "new poor."

Can we end poverty?

Define poverty as living on $1.90 a day or less. Now imagine that governments could put $1.91 in every poor person's pocket with little effort and minimal waste. Poverty is finished. Of course, things are more complicated than that. But you get a sense of where modern social policy is going—and what will soon be possible.

To start with, there is a budding consensus on what reduces poverty: it is the combination of fast and sustained economic growth (more jobs), stable consumer prices (no inflation), and targeted redistribution (subsidies only to the poor). On those three fronts, developing countries are beginning to make real progress.

So, where will poverty fighters focus next? First, on better jobs. What matters to reduce poverty is not just jobs, but how productive that employment is. This highlights the need for a broad agenda of reforms to make an economy more competitive. It also points toward something much closer to the individual: skills, both cognitive (e.g., critical thinking or communication ability) and noncognitive (e.g., attitude toward newness or sense of responsibility).

Second, poverty fighters will target projects that augment human opportunity. As will be explained next, it is now possible to measure how important personal circumstances—like skin color, birthplace, or gender—are in a child's probability of accessing the services—like education, clean water, or the Internet—necessary to succeed in life. That measure, called the Human Opportunity Index, has opened the door for policymakers to focus not just on giving everybody the same rewards but also the same chances, not just on equality but on equity. A few countries, mostly in Latin America, now evaluate existing social programs, and design new ones, with equality of opportunity in mind. Others will follow.

And third, greater focus will be put on lowering social risk and enhancing social protection. A few quarters of recession, a sudden inflationary spike, or a natural disaster, and poverty counts skyrocket—and stay sky-high for years. The technology to protect the middle class from slipping into poverty, and the poor from sinking even deeper, is still rudimentary in the developing world. Just think of the scant coverage of unemployment insurance.

But the real breakthrough is that to raise productivity, expand opportunity, or reduce risk, you now have a power tool: direct cash transfers. Most developing countries (thirty-five of them in Africa) have, over the last twenty years, set up logistical mechanisms to send money directly to the poor—mainly through debit cards and cell phones. Initially, the emphasis was on the conditions attached to the transfer, such as keeping your child in school or visiting a clinic if you were pregnant. It soon became clear that the value of these programs was to be found less in their conditions than in the fact that they forced government agencies to know the poor by name. Now we know where they live, how much they earn, and how many kids they have.[12]

That kind of state–citizen relationship is transforming social policy. Think of the massive amount of information it is generating in real time—how much things actually cost, what people really prefer, what impact government is having, what remains to be done. This is helping improve the quality of expenditures, that is, better targeting, design, efficiency, fairness, and, ultimately, results. It also helps deal with shocks like the global crisis (have you ever wondered why there was no social explosion in Mexico when the US economy nose-dived in early 2009?). Sure, giving away taxpayers' money was bound to cause debate (how do you know you are not financing bums?). But so far, direct transfers have survived political transitions, from Left to Right (Chile) and from Right to Left (El Salvador). The debate has been about doing transfers well, not about abandoning them.

A final point. For all the promise of new poverty-reduction techniques, just getting everybody in the developing world over the $1.90-per-day threshold would be no moral success. (To understand why, try to picture your life on a $1.90-per-day budget; really, do it). But it would be a very good beginning.

Is there a way to measure human opportunity?

Imagine a country where your future does not depend on where you come from, how much your family owns, what color your skin is, or whether you are male or female. Imagine if personal circumstances, those over which you have no control or responsibility, were irrelevant to your opportunities and to your children's opportunities. And imagine if there was a statistical tool to guide governments in making that a reality. There is. It was created in 2008 by a consortium of researchers sponsored by the World Bank. It is called the Human Opportunity Index (HOI) and it may one day turn social policy upside down.[13]

The HOI calculates how personal circumstances (e.g., birthplace, wealth, race, or gender) impact the probability a child has of accessing the services that are necessary to succeed in life (e.g., timely education, basic health, or access to electricity). When it was first applied to Latin America (to a dataset representing two hundred million children), the findings were eye-opening: behind the region's famously unequal distribution of development outcomes (among them income, land ownership, and educational attainment), there is an even larger inequality of development opportunities. Not only are the rewards unequal, so too are the chances. The problem is not just about equality; it is about equity too—the playing field is uneven from the start.

Efforts have been made to measure human opportunity in a selection of developed and developing countries (some in Africa). And within countries, comparisons were made across states and cities. What have we learned? Three things. First, there is now a way out of the endless, acrimonious debate over inequality—a debate that has polarized politics in the developing world (and in much of the developed one as well). Should governments try to redistribute wealth or to protect private property rights? Should they try to enforce social justice or contracts? We will never reach universal agreement on those issues. But the idea of giving people equal opportunity early in life, whatever their socioeconomic background, is embraced across the political spectrum—as a matter of fairness for the Left and as a matter of personal effort for the Right.

Second, the HOI, combined with the massive improvement in the quality of household surveys over the past decade, will make it possible to redirect social policy toward equity (where there is political consensus) and away from equality (where there is not). How? Many existing social policies and programs are already equity enhancing. But focusing on equity reveals new points of emphasis along the individual's life cycle. Early interventions, from pregnancy monitoring and professionally assisted births, to toddlers' nutrition and neurological development, get a new sense of priority. So does preschool access (such as prekindergarten social interaction) and primary school achievement (such as reading standards and critical thinking). Physical security, reproductive education, mentoring, and talent screening in adolescents—all areas that are often overlooked—gain new relevance. A battery of legal and institutional preconditions becomes sine qua non, from birth certificates, voter registration, and property titles, to the enforcement of anti-discrimination, antitrust, and access-to-information laws. And blanket subsidies, which at the margin are consumed by those who do not need them (free public college education for the rich, to name one), turn into opportunity-wasting aberrations. If anything else, the quest for equity will lead to a final push in the long process of subsidy focalization and will spell the endgame for a way of giving out public assistance that was blind to the needs of the recipient—a way that was intrinsically unfair.

And third, there is a personal circumstance that seems to dominate all others. It is not your race or gender or birthplace or family wealth. Those are important, of course. But the single most powerful determinant of your chances in life appears to be your mother's education—not your father's, but your mother's. We don't quite know exactly why. It may have to do with effective rearing time (kids just spend more time with their moms than with anybody else). It may be peer pressure among mothers (if my friend's child already reads, mine will read too). Or it may be the way women learn and communicate (that careful attention to detail). Whatever the reason, educating girls today enhances equity for all tomorrow.

Why are statistics so important in ending poverty?

The more you know about your enemy, the easier it is to beat it. This is true for wars against armies, diseases, or corruption—good information will tell you where to best deploy your soldiers, doctors, and auditors. The same happens in the fight against poverty. You want your resources to go where they help the poor the most. For that you need accurate, frequent, timely, comprehensive, comparable, consistent, and accessible data. And that is exactly what we are beginning to get. In fact, data is transforming the development profession—you can call it the revenge of the statisticians.

Here is how that transformation is happening. First, the funding of multilateral institutions—like the World Bank—is now more closely linked to the results they promise to achieve. To get money from taxpayers, they have to commit to specific "goals." *How much* will infant mortality fall? *How many* children will be vaccinated? *How many* girls will learn to read and write? *What proportion* of women will have access to contraceptives? *By when?* All this is creating a culture of monitoring and evaluation—"M & E," in development parlance—that is bringing light to what works and what does not work. For that, you need data.

Second, data is doing to public subsidies today what privatization did to public enterprises two decades ago: it is lifting the veil of inefficiency. With better household surveys, we can identify who exactly benefits from every dollar the government spends—not surprisingly, this is called "benefit incidence analysis." Take education. Most developing countries spend more bankrolling free public universities than building primary schools. But the main beneficiaries of that subsidized college education are the rich (who *can* pay tuition), not the poor (who *cannot*). You see the inefficiency? The same applies for subsidies to gasoline (who owns cars?), electricity (who has larger houses?), or pensions (who has formal jobs?). Statistics lets you quantify this madness—and argue that the money should be redirected toward those who really need it.

Third, better data is allowing us to focus on poor people's noncognitive skills. You see, whether you get a good job—or any job—does not only depend on how many exams you pass, how much you know, or what your IQ is. It also depends on things like how conscientious you are, how you react to new experiences, or how well you interact with others—think of it as the "noncognitive" side of your resume. Is it better to be smarter or to be on time? To know more or to listen more? To be trained or to be trainable? Household surveys are beginning to gather information that will, one day, allow us to answer those questions—Peru is a leader in this among emerging economies. And when we get the answers, we will be able to design educational curricula to teach not just the concepts but also the behaviors that make people more productive.

Fourth, it is possible to determine how personal circumstances affect human opportunity. We all know that children have no control or responsibility over their gender, skin color, birthplace, or parents' income. And yet, those kinds of circumstances are sure-shot predictors of a child's access to vaccinations, potable water, kindergarten, the Internet, and many other platforms without which her probability of success is close to nil—well before she can make any decision by herself. This can now be measured, something that was impossible only a few years ago. The measure is called the Human Opportunity Index (see above), and it is beginning to change how social policy is designed.

Finally, we have broken the taboo of experimenting with people. It is no longer unusual for researchers to walk into a slum, offer childcare to a sample of mothers, and then monitor whether they work outside the home more hours than those with no child care at all. (FYI: They don't always do.) This type of "randomized controlled trial" is proving really useful to assess what policies and what projects work best—and which are a waste of time and money. From giving cheap fertilizer to farmers to making cheap loans to female micro-entrepreneurs, you can evaluate anything, as long as you have—or create—the data.

By now, you are probably wondering where all this data is going to come from. Isn't it true that most national statistical offices in the developing world are somewhere between weak and very weak? After all, those all-important household surveys, when they exist, get published years after they are collected. Millions are rightly being spent to upgrade statistical capacity. But it takes a long, long while before you see results—which explains why politicians rarely care about it.

Is there a shortcut? Is there a fast way to get the data we need to help the poor? Yes, and it is probably sitting in your pocket, in your purse, or on your belt. It is your cell phone. It turns out that people will happily sign up to answer a couple of short phone surveys a month in exchange for "free minutes" of phone use. How many minutes? On average less than five dollars' worth of minutes per month. (Yes, that's how cheap we all are.) This is a bargain because you don't have to call more than one-tenth of 1 percent of your population to get a good reading of how your country is doing.

As the use of cellular telephony expands among the poor—at flash speed in places like Kenya—the possibility of turning them into data sources becomes real. In fact, some of this is already happening in Latin America and may soon catch on in Africa. Others will surely follow. How ironic that, in the end, the war against poverty may be won when those who try to help the poor get to *literally* listen to them.

Do we know the real impact of government interventions?

Imagine an average developing country whose government decides to pay for the bus tickets of all its high school students. If it can afford it, what would be wrong with that? It would make it easier for teenagers, especially those of modest means, to attend school and graduate. It would also make them—and their parents—much happier. That would surely be the *outcome* of the new policy, and many people would support it. But wait. What would be the *impact*? That is, what would happen now that would not have happened if the policy had not been adopted? Well, very likely, most teenagers would now consume more beer—yes, the new subsidy will free them from using their own bus money to commute and, you know, they would use it for what they like best—and their parents least. You get the point: *outcome* is not the same as *impact*. You may support the former but hate the latter.

It gets better. A mildly corrupt president has enough public funds to build a school or to buy jewelry for his new wife, but not both. Just when he was grudgingly going to do the right thing, along comes a well-intentioned international development bank that wants to promote education by making loans to build schools. The president, full of smiles, signs the loan in front of the cameras and the school is built. *Outcome* of the bank's intervention: more classrooms. *Impact*: more bling for the first lady. By financing the school, the bank actually funded corruption.

You see, you can analyze the impact of almost everything governments try to do—from bailing out their banking systems to creating jobs to protecting the environment. And, handy at times of austerity, you can do the same for whatever governments stop doing—say, paying generous pension benefits. In fact, the technology for assessing the *impact* of economic policy has been around for years—economists love it, if only to prove how simple-minded some politicians can be. But it was rarely used outside rich countries. Now it is. What caused the change? Data.

To detect impact, we need to know what governments, people, and enterprises do with their money—we need to know their budgets. In advanced countries that is not a problem—if you live in a developed economy, chances are that consumer research companies already know more about your spending habits than you do. And in those economies, governments publish their fiscal budgets and enterprises file their tax returns. The novelty is that the same is beginning to happen in the developing world.[14] Recent improvements in household and industrial surveys are providing better, more comprehensive, and more frequent readings of how firms and people—including the poor—allocate their resources. Credit-rating agencies and watchdog NGOs are doing the equivalent to governments by pushing them to open up their books. Today, the fiscal accounts of Chile, Brazil, Mexico, Slovenia, South Africa, Sri Lanka, and many others are posted on the Web. They are far from perfect and not always easy to understand. But the trend is clear.

So, armed with numbers, impact analysis is becoming a game changer in the development profession. Not only is it telling us what government action really does—as compared with what it means to do—it also tells us who will

win and who will lose with it. Reforms become easier once
you know who will support them, who will oppose them,
and who should be compensated. Take the case of subsidies that keep gasoline prices low. The poor use public
transportation, and doing away with subsidies on gasoline
will make it harder for them to get to work. Since they *need*
to work, they may cut back on, say, preventive healthcare
for their children (how about that for an impact?). You will
be forced to compensate them. But it is the rich who drive
the big cars. When you pay to make gasoline cheaper for
the well-off, you are in effect paying for the wine, gym
membership, cable TV, or whatever else they do with the
cash they do not have to leave at the gas station. (You think
this is far-fetched? There is a Latin American country that
spends more on subsidizing gasoline for the wealthiest
20 percent of its population than on all its social programs
put together.) Now you have a map of where the resistance
to reform stems from and can figure out how to overcome
it. You can also use the map to redress gross injustices—to
bring equity back on the agenda, if you will.

Whether reforms follow or not, uncovering the true
meaning of what our leaders do has irresistible appeal
in and of itself. No wonder impact analysis has become
almost an academic obsession to the new generation of
economists—especially those that want to change the
world (which is most of them). Just the World Bank alone
has invested twenty million dollars of European donors'
money in finding the impact that its projects will actually
have on poverty—*before* they are launched. Other institutions are doing the same. The point is that the technical
reasons that kept us blind to the real effects of policies and
programs exist no longer.

But will impact analysis change the way policies are
made in practice? Will evidence rule politics? Slowly, it
will. As democracy takes hold, education spreads, and

information flows faster, farther, and cheaper; even poor countries will see change in the political discourse—some, in Africa, are seeing it already. Of course, catchy slogans will have to be spun to communicate dry statistics to voters. That's not trivial, but it's certainly doable. We will all be better off for it.[15]

Can cheap oil hurt the poor?

After four years of hovering at about a hundred dollars per barrel, the price of oil suddenly collapsed in July 2014—and is expected to stay at seventy dollars or less for the rest of this decade. Both more supply and less demand are behind the change: large producers in the Arabian Peninsula keep pumping apace, the United States is "fracking" away at its shale reserves, and China's economic growth is slowing down—all at the same time. This has sent economists rushing to assess what cheap oil means for the global economy. Depending on the model they use and the assumptions they make, they estimate a net stimulus that ranges from small to very small. But, behind the word "net" lies a wide spectrum of gains, pains, people, and policies.

Simulations by the World Bank and others suggest that, *everything else equal*, the global economy can grow a tenth of 1 percent faster if oil prices stay a third below their average level of 2014. As a group, rich countries would benefit more than developing ones—think of less expensive energy helping with Europe's recovery. Oil exporters—like Nigeria, Russia, and Venezuela—stand to lose a great deal, while oil importers—like China, India, and Japan—will gain a bit. And growth in oil-rich regions like the Middle East, Central Asia, and West Africa may decline rather sharply—by 2 or more percentage points.

So far, so predictable. What makes the World Bank team's simulation interesting is that even among oil exporters the impact will vary a lot. The reason is that they are not all equally prepared to cope with the fall in oil prices—not all of them used well the "good times" of hundred-dollar-plus a barrel. This is a key point: the effect of cheaper oil on any one country—and on its people—depends not just on whether it sells petroleum or not but, if it does, also on whether it has created the external and fiscal "buffers" to cushion a plunge in prices. The typical buffers are little or no foreign debt, large reserves of foreign currency, balanced fiscal budgets, sovereign wealth funds, and flexible public expenditures. While not perfect, Colombia, Malaysia, and Norway are examples of that.

Why are those macroeconomic buffers so important? *Because they help protect the poor*. Without buffers, an abrupt loss of export earnings means slower or negative growth, higher inflation, and less government revenue—that is, fewer jobs, pricier food, and less social assistance. In other words, for unprepared oil-exporting countries, cheaper oil means more poverty. At present, there are some seven hundred million people in such countries—eighty million of whom already live on $1.90 a day or less.

Of course, unlike simulations, in the real world "everything else" does not stay equal. Low prices discourage new investments in exploration, especially for shale oil, something that may over time raise prices; by some projections, oil prices could recover their 2014 level as early as 2019. More to the point, politicians and policymakers can plan for and react to shocks, especially if they happen to lead an oil-exporting country and care about poverty. They can secure loans years in advance, delay investment projects, cut subsidies to the rich, shore up banks, and identify people and industries that will suffer the most. Above all, they can make sure that they do not waste the shock. A major change in your external environment can help you tackle long-neglected internal

reforms. This is a great time, for example, to remove subsidies to fossil fuel or to make life easier for industries
that can export something other than oil. It is also high
time to change the behaviors that make your economy
buffer-less: fiscal budgets that are built on overoptimistic price projections, public spending that is borderline
extravagant, pledges of oil revenue to overborrow, and
political reluctance to create rainy-day funds. Whether
your country sells or buys oil, whether it is rich or poor, a
slump in international oil prices can be turned into a fine
development opportunity.

4

INCLUSION

THOSE WHO ARE ALWAYS LEFT BEHIND

Will we ever reach gender parity?

If it could rid itself of gender discrimination, the average developing country would see its economy grow at least 2 percentage points faster every year. That would generate enough public resources to double the size of most social protection programs, fund prekindergarten education for all children, or maintain just about every road. So, if it is so important, why aren't we making progress toward gender parity? Actually, we are—but not nearly enough. The problem is best stated in four propositions.

Proposition One: *There has never been a better time to be a woman.* Women have slowly gained access to employment, education, property, credit, justice, contraceptives, and power. Over the past three decades alone, female participation in the labor force has increased by 10 percentage points; today, six of every ten women work outside their homes. Except for West Africa, fertility rates—the number of babies born per mother—have fallen everywhere. Half a century ago, the average Latin American mother had more than six children (yes, really); now she barely has two. Many countries report higher school enrollment rates for girls than boys, especially in upper grades. Ditto for university graduation rates. Political representation has never been larger—the proportion of female parliamentarians is larger in Rwanda than in Sweden. And yet . . .

Proposition Two: *Our daughters' world can, should, and probably will be better than our sisters'*. It is true that access has vastly improved. The issue now is what happens after access. More women join the labor force but, once there, become "occupationally segregated"—stuck in lower productivity, lower technology jobs. Their general absence from the ICT industry is a conspicuous example. They get title to their homes, but find local police slow in enforcing their ownership when no-longer-welcome partners refuse to leave. They have fewer children, but they cannot afford childcare. They are present in parliament, but their votes rarely swing legislation. And every year six million of them go "missing" from the demographic radar—terminated by parents who prefer sons to daughters, or killed by lack of medical care when giving birth. You get the picture.

Proposition Three: *Treating women fairly would make everyone richer*. Imagine an economy in which half of all machines were misplaced: tractors were sent to hospitals, brain scanners to barbershops, hair dryers to construction sites, cranes to car factories, and crash-test dummies to farms. To make the misallocation worse, imagine that some of your best and most powerful computers are kept locked in a depot. Now imagine that you undo this madness. Just letting your assets go where they can be most useful would make you a lot more productive. Well, what is true for physical assets is true for human ones too. Removing the barriers that keep women from doing the jobs they are best at will expand the economy's production capacity—even at the same level of investment. It will also save you from being wiped out by your competitors in the global market—how do you expect to succeed if you only deploy half your brainpower? Gender parity is not only a moral priority, it is also smart economics.

Proposition Four: *Better policies and bigger projects will not by themselves achieve gender parity—we also need cultural change.* Plenty of new laws and institutions have been put in place, and billions of dollars have been spent, across the developing world to ensure equal opportunities for women, especially in the past ten years. Most of it has been pretty successful. (For a top-of-the-line example of the benefits that property titles brought to Peruvian women living in the slums outside of Lima, go to http://bit.ly/12yu2OI.) Some long-postponed or long-incomplete reforms are still necessary: we still need to put a doctor at every birth; provide childcare to poor mothers; pay for disadvantaged girls to finish high school; teach youngsters about reproductive health; make family planning free to all; and see affirmative action through in politics, courts, and unions. But real change will come about only when gender becomes as integral and natural to development as, say, environmental protection or fiscal transparency.

Today, nobody would construct a dam or a highway without thinking of its environmental impact. And in most countries crooked civil servants lose their jobs—and their freedom—if they are exposed. But only three decades ago, we rarely spoke about pollution or corruption. What changed? *People* did, especially young people. A mix of social activism and public education campaigns convinced a new generation to do the right thing and to vote accordingly. Politicians and their technocrats listened. Think of Greenpeace in the 1980s reaching into kindergartens with its "Be Kind to Earth" message. Those kids are now adults and would think twice before backing a party that stands for forest cutting, whale killing, or SUV driving. The time has come for the same to happen to gender parity. Cultures will need to change and value women and men equally. And once again it will be our children who lead the way.

Has globalization helped or hurt women?

The idea sounded good. Faced with competition from cheap imports, employers would ditch their prejudices and start hiring workers strictly for their skills—irrespective of gender. Foreign investors would go in and set up corporations eager to recruit the best local talent—whatever the sex. They would bring new technologies that would require less brawn and more brain to operate—cutting into men's physical advantage. A college degree would become a lot more valuable, favoring the legions of women that had earned one—mostly because they had been discriminated out of the labor force. Banks from other countries would offer loans to our biggest firms, forcing domestic banks to focus on our smaller enterprises—a business segment where women are overrepresented. Even social norms would change when we established more contact with the rest of the world, when we saw that other societies do just fine despite having female leaders and female drivers. Globalization—that is, freer movement of people, money, goods, and ideas across borders—was bound to do wonders for gender parity. That was the early 1980s. Almost forty years later, it's fair to ask: Did it happen?

New research shows mixed results.[1] In countries where new industries emerged, women found more employment opportunities—think of Mexico's *maquiladoras*. But they remained "occupationally segregated," that is, unable to branch out into the better paying jobs—like computer programming. And in economies with little or no manufacturing—like most of Africa—most women remained stuck in subsistence farming. Yes, their families were paid more for their crops thanks to the rise in the international prices of commodities, but the money continued to be controlled by their husbands. And still today, women do not work in the booming oil, gas, or mining fields.

This also puts a question mark on graduate education. There is little evidence—granted, it is difficult to collect—that globalization tore down the walls that kept women out of the professions or at a low rank. The image of the gender-blind foreign manager or foreign client may have proved too optimistic. Female accountants, doctors, and architects rarely operate solo, and the firms, hospitals, or studios where they work face less competition from abroad—and therefore less incentive to change. If you don't believe so, just visit the website of any of the major Latin American law firms, check the gender balance of their partner list, and, after you recover from the shock, remember that this is the region of the developing world where women have made the most progress.

How about finance? What did the free flow of capital in and out of countries do for gender? It certainly opened the door to more credit for women, but only in countries that also took care of the legalities that make female borrowers less attractive—things like lack of title to their houses or a clear claim to inherited land. It expanded banking services, giving women a safer way to save, receive remittances, and make payments. More subtly, financial globalization forced governments to keep inflation low—if they don't, investors quickly take their money abroad. Women have been big beneficiaries of this, as it is they who do the shopping for their families.

Ironically, where globalization may have had the largest gender impact is at home—literally. As women got more jobs and bigger incomes, the power balance within the household shifted. In places where it happened, the "feminization" of export industries raised the cost of forcing women to stay at home to care for children and the elderly—when Mom or Big Sister can make a decent wage outside the house, their time suddenly becomes conspicuously valuable to the whole family. The same happens to female entrepreneurs who gain access to credit. Not to mention that when the breadwinner in the house is a female, more is spent on children's food and education. (There are plenty of studies showing this, even across countries that are culturally very different from each other, like Ghana, Brazil, China, and India.)[2]

Does this all mean that globalization did not help women? No, it did. By raising income levels throughout the economy, it helped everybody—men *and* women. Things, of course, vary a lot from country to country and from city to village, but on the whole globalization made people richer. What the opening of frontiers has not really done is to promote *gender parity*, that is, to end—or at least push back—discrimination. This raises a worrisome question: Were gender disparities *exacerbated* by freer movement of goods and capital? They may have been, especially in agriculture-based societies where the cultural norms inside the household are particularly strong. The lesson is simple: foreign influence by itself does not change who we are or how we treat each other.

Impact evaluation: A woman's best friend?

Since the early 1900s, the world celebrates International Women's Day each March. In the earlier years, there was not much to "celebrate." Today, there is. The past three decades have witnessed real progress toward gender equity.[3] Women have gained access to education, healthcare, jobs, land, and other assets that were once out of reach. They now live twenty years longer than they did in

1960. Girls are as likely as boys to go to primary school in just about every country—and in sixty of those countries there are more young women in universities than men. And over half a billion women have joined the labor force. Nobody can deny that our sisters have more opportunities than our mothers and fewer than our daughters.

Of course, *progress toward* gender equity is not the same as gender equity itself. In Malawi, a female farmer produces a quarter less per hectare than a man—mainly because she can't access the same inputs. A mother in Afghanistan has a one in thirty-two chance of dying while giving birth. Women entrepreneurs in Bangladesh make twelve cents for every dollar men make. And you only have to watch the news to see that women are underrepresented in politics, business, and many professions. (Don't think this is a poor-country problem: female workers in Germany make sixty-two cents for every Euro men make.)

This sense of insufficient progress, of being halfway across the river, is frustrating: many smart people and well-meaning institutions have worked for a long time on policies, programs, and projects to advance the cause of women. They have spent billions of dollars. The results have, on the whole, been underwhelming, mostly because cultural norms still play a big role and may be hard to change. Can those committed champions get more for their efforts to level the playing field for women? Can we accelerate the march toward gender-blind societies? Yes, we can. The key is to tell apart what works from what doesn't—and invest more in the former. The tool to do just that is called "impact evaluation."

One crude way to understand an impact evaluation is to think of it as a medical trial: to know whether a new pill works, you select two groups of people *at random*, one takes the pill ("the treatment," in technical parlance) and the other doesn't (they are the "control group"). You then compare how the two groups react and figure out what the pill actually did. Well, you can apply the same principle to the world's toughest gender problems, and what you learn is pretty amazing.

Here are some examples. A team of researchers looked at the impact of reserving local government positions for women in India in one-third of the electoral districts, *randomly* selected. This made a huge difference. Compared with other districts, in the selected third, it was more likely that public investment was aligned with female preferences, for crime against women to be reported, and for parents to send their daughters to school.[4]

When Rwanda piloted a land-registration system, it made sure that women received rights equal to men and, in particular, equal to their husbands.[5] The system initially covered only a few rural areas. So, it was easy to compare households living just inside the borders of those areas with those living just outside—that is, to compare neighbors who had received "the treatment" with others who had not. It turns out that when female farmers feel that their property rights are secured, they increase their investment twice as much as men. In other words, if you want them to produce more, give them clear titles to what is theirs, and everyone will be better off.

In Uganda, a program to empower adolescent girls through mentoring, reproductive education, and job skills proved, through an impact evaluation, to be a real game-changer: those who participated in the program became a third more likely to find work and a quarter less likely to get pregnant—while their odds of being raped fell from one in five to almost zero.[6]

But the beauty of impact evaluations is that they also show what *doesn't* work—even things that you were *sure* would help women. Take training for female business owners, a popular way to try to help them prosper. What can be wrong with that? Nothing, except that, in most cases, it makes little or no difference for the bottom-line of women-owned enterprises. A review of evaluations of this kind of training in places like Pakistan, Peru, and Tanzania suggests that it does not yield great value for money.[7]

Granted, whether something works—or doesn't—in a certain community at a certain time does not mean that it will work—or fail—everywhere later on. You can't easily generalize the results of an impact evaluation. But you can distill lessons, compare experiences, debunk myths, spot problems, and test solutions. In other words, you learn. And the accumulated knowledge makes you more effective next time around. It is no surprise that many organizations—from donors and academia to NGOs and multilateral banks—are currently dedicated to using impact evaluations to attack some of the most urgent challenges in economic development. Reaching gender equity should be at the top of their list—not just on Women's Day, but every day.[8]

How did average housewives become the greatest generation of Argentine women?

She was born in 1930. The child of poor European immigrants, she married the son of other poor European immigrants. They settled in one of Buenos Aires' many *barrios*, those aspiring working-class neighborhoods where the children of immigrants used to settle. A life as a housewife would follow—husband, kids, cooking, church, an omnipresent TV set. Her story was unremarkable. There were millions of Argentine women just like her. And yet, Alicia Tamburelli—that's her name—and her generation would do something amazing, a dare that would define history, something that lesser leaders would deem impossible. From the anonymity of their kitchens, and for decades on end, they managed to protect their families from the perennial failure of their country's political class.

Start in 1947. Women were "given" the right to vote. And they voted with gusto. But soon enough, democracy disappeared. Or, rather, it became intermittent, with years of military dictators in shiny boots who didn't talk much, followed by sleek civilians who talked a lot. Somehow, from the *barrio*, they all looked the same, though—distant, rich, arrogant, always shouting at you, always waving that index finger. Definitely not the kind of people Ms. Tamburelli wanted her children to mingle with, let alone become.

Had those leaders at least been competent, it would have been easier to put up with them. But what a mess they made. They couldn't keep prices stable—so inflation kept housewives like Alicia walking from grocery shop to grocery shop, always hopeful for a lower price. They couldn't decide whether private businesses—especially those big foreign ones—were a good thing or a bad thing, so there were never enough jobs. Some years, the economy was open and full of cheap imported radios, refrigerators, and cars. And some years it was closed, so there was no way to get parts to fix the radios, refrigerators, and cars when they broke down. At times, banks would pay a lot for your deposits, and at times they would just refuse to return your money—"A new government policy, sorry." If that was not tough enough, pensions were sometimes "pay-as-you-go" (meaning the government takes your money, spends it, and pays you whatever it wants when you retire) and sometimes "capitalized" (meaning you are on your own). What to do? How do you survive so much economic uncertainty, Ms. Tamburelli? Very easy. Buy only what you need, use the rest to buy US dollars, and keep them under your mattress—literally. In other words, these women became fine macroeconomists.

How about public services, things like the electricity, gas, and transportation that any family needs? Well, some decades they were truly "public," and ridiculously cheap, but rarely worked. (Alicia and her neighbors were so happy when she was the first to get a phone line—only after five years on the waiting list.) Some decades the services were privatized. That meant that a rich family owned them and charged a fortune for them, but the supply was plentiful—and there was even a number to call and, mostly inconsequentially, complain. And some decades, it wasn't clear who owned what, who was responsible for what, and who paid for what. How do you live like that? You plan for the worst possible service—blackouts, cut-offs, strikes, and accidents. If these things don't happen, great. If they do, you deal with it and move on.

You see, there was almost nothing those incompetent politicians could do that this great generation of women could not handle—almost. The fact is that Argentine governments never managed to keep people safe. For a while, they even went to war with their own country—"disappearing" some thirty thousand of their own citizens. And they always failed to control, even less punish, crime. Ms. Tamburelli would proudly tell you that every asset in her family—the house, the car, the wallets—had been robbed at least once and that she never bothered to report it to the police—she knew better. Impunity became a way of life. You just triple-lock the doors, don't walk in the dark, and carry no jewelry. More than anything, you pray that your kids would each night come home safe.

For one thing was clear: to these women, their kids—and the kids of their kids—were the center of life. That's where they drew the line. They would do anything to protect them against the incompetent madness of the politicians.

That included letting their children go, letting them migrate in search of a better place. About two million did and now live abroad. Weren't those families sadly separated? Yes, but they were preserved.

So, Alicia, how did you and the ladies from your generation carry on? Is there any advice for the next lot? Is there a "Tamburelli doctrine"? There is, and it goes more or less like this: Never miss a day of work. All debts are bad. No expenditure is more important than your children's education. Keep your hands always clean. And never expect anything good from the government. Brilliant.

Alicia Tamburelli died on February 17, 2012, aged eighty-one. She was one in a legion of Argentine women who are coming to the end, triumphant in their anonymity.

Why do the poor complain so little?

You are visiting a poor village somewhere in the developing world. No paved roads, no electricity, no running water, no clinic, and only a thatch-roofed shack for a school. You soon hear stories of malnutrition, disease, and illiteracy—all symptoms of no or lousy public services. But you know this is a country booming with oil, gas, and minerals. So the inevitable question comes to your mind: Why don't these people organize and demand more from their government?

In the past, it was easy to attribute the seeming passivity of the poor to a lack of political freedom—it is not for nothing that "poverty" and "repression" are closely associated words. The spread of democracy, especially over the past two decades, has given the poor a new voice. But they have used it much less than one would expect. Yes, from South America to South Asia, you see angry demonstrations when governments try to cut subsidies to fuel, bread, or fertilizer. But why not complain about things like the terrible quality of primary education, preventable child mortality, or corrupt civil servants? And what of the billions of oil dollars the government may have collected over the years but can't account for? Rarely do you see those kinds of demonstrations.

The common explanation these days has to do with information—the poor just don't know how bad the performance of public schools, hospitals, and bureaucrats is. They may not even know how much money their government gets from selling the country's natural resources. So official donors, development banks, and NGOs have put a lot of effort in providing the poor information about the quality of public services. The idea makes sense: once aware of the gravity of the problem, people will pressure their politicians to do something about it. The proliferation of communication technology—especially cell phones—has made it all that easier.

Has it worked? Do better informed poor people demand better government? The evidence is mixed. New research shows widely different results across countries and across services. Using a pretty scientific method—called randomized controlled trials—it has been possible to compare how social groups react (or not) when faced with the reality that their leaders are underserving them. For example, in Uganda, facilitating meetings between communities and their public healthcare workers led to better performance by the latter—and fewer children dying.[9] But showing parents in rural Kenya how shamefully low their children scored on standardized tests made little difference in parental involvement with the local school.[10] Training community volunteers to hold remedial, after-school reading camps in India improved the reading skills of the children who attended.[11] But a heart-wrenching movie about Peruvian second-graders trying to read—and failing at it—caused only a short-lived public outcry.[12] For almost every case where information led to activism, you will find one where it didn't. Why?

Because information is a necessary but not sufficient condition for people—especially poor people—to react. Even when the information is easy to understand—"a second-grader should read at least sixty words per minute"—and its content is bad enough to produce outrage—"only ten percent of our second-graders can read sixty words per minute"—people may still not demand reform. To start with, it is easier to take individual than collective action; when parents in Benin were informed about the status of their local schools, many made an extra effort to pay for private tutoring rather than together complaining to the principal. Then there is the question of patronage: you may forgive your long-serving member of parliament for doing nothing about the village's clinic because he has been good at providing government jobs to the village's folk. Culture plays a big role too: different societies care differently about different issues. And, even when you care deeply, you may not think you are able to deal with or be responsible for the problem ("I do my job, that school principal should do his!").

All that rings true. But perhaps the most promising explanation comes from something called "behavioral economics." This involves experiments designed to understand why people do things that make no sense or neglect doing what would benefit them.[13] One increasingly common finding is that human beings seem to have a limited mental "bandwidth"—think of it as your attention span when it comes to economic decisions—and that poverty can occupy most of it. When your preoccupation today—and yesterday and tomorrow—is getting enough food for your family to eat, you can be excused for not worrying too much about forming a civic movement to reform public education, healthcare, or the fiscal budget.

Yes, you know that it is important, and would love to do something about it, but you just can't focus on it right now. That does not ignore the many heroes of social change who came from abject poverty. But it confirms what sounds obvious: information is power as long as you have the possibility to act on it. It would also suggest that richer societies hold their governments more closely accountable. Economic development and citizen activism feed on each other.

Why is early childhood development so difficult?

In 2011, I met a very poor teenage mother in a slum outside Maputo, the capital of Mozambique (per capita income: less than two dollars a day). She was carrying a baby whom she had given birth to a few weeks before—inside of her house, with no medical assistance. Of course, the child had no birth certificate, and his mother was unlikely to try to get one—she could not afford the cost of the bus ride to a registration center. Result: her son is pretty much condemned to a life of poverty. He will never have a property title, be part of a contract, hold a license, join a union, register for college, or vote in an election. Technically, he will not exist. He won't be alone: it is estimated that two of every three African children do not exist either. They also have no birth certificate.

How come something so apparently trivial that occurs so early in life—like not having a piece of paper that confirms who you are—can hurt you so badly and so permanently? Well, it turns out that your chances to succeed in life are quickly spoiled by things that happen long before you arrive in a school, if you ever do. And even if those things don't happen, it is *still* not certain that you will make it. Crazy, isn't it? Welcome to the drama, the frustration, the promise, and the beauty of early childhood development.

Nutrition is the best example of how this works. We do not know for how long exactly an infant needs to be undernourished before she starts to lose cognitive capacity (some scientists say a month is enough). What we know for sure is that a lack of iodine or iron, and sheer stunting, before the age of two will probably shave some 10 points off your IQ—forever. (Remember, the average person's IQ is only 100). With that kind of intellectual handicap, the odds are that you will not get a good job, ever. Your luck will be all but sealed from the beginning, in slow motion, right in front of the eyes of parents, governments, and donors. In fact, malnourishment is easy to detect: if a baby does not grow at least 24 centimeters in her first twelve months, you know immediately there is a problem—regardless of race, family history, or geographic location. What is less obvious is that more food may still not solve your nutritional problem. If your child has no potable water, sanitation, hygiene, or vaccinations, she is bound to lose nutrients anyway.

The point is that early childhood development is an all-or-nothing business. Even with good nutrition, the construction of the brain—the computer of the future worker, if you will—is easily derailed. The speed at which cells connect with each other in the brain—its "plasticity" in the technical lingo—peaks during your first year of life. (It peaks at seven hundred connections per second, if you want to know.) After that, it begins to slow down. So, if the process is interrupted or delayed by external "stresses"—things like hunger, disease, neglect, violence, or orphanhood—during your first year, you miss the most trainable moment of your existence. It will take a lot of money and a lot of luck to catch up later. (If you want to hear this from one of the world's leading experts, you can view a 2010 lecture by Dr. Jack Shonkoff, the director of the Center on the Developing Child at Harvard, at http://bit.ly/Pedorh.)

That explains the enormous value of preschool education—and the huge disadvantage in missing it. By the time a child gets to first grade—usually by the age of five—much of her cognitive, motor, sensory, and social skills are on a difficult-to-change trajectory. That is why, when you compare two children arriving for their very first day of class, one who has been exposed to systematic, continuous, and positive stimulation, and one who has not, the difference between their learning abilities is the transportation equivalent of the difference between a car and a horse. Mind you, we are not talking about "formal" preschool education. Even if it is your father reading to you every night, the local shopkeeper letting you count the candies, or your community's priest telling you about good behavior, it is early, regular training in reasoning and communication that matters.

Now the child is in school. How soon can we know whether she'll make it or not? Sadly, very soon. If by the end of second grade she cannot read at least sixty words per minute, it is almost certain that she will not finish sixth grade on time—in turn a sure-shot predictor of whether she will attend college. What's so magic about reading sixty words per minute when you are a seven-year-old? At slower reading speeds you lose the meaning of the sentence. In other words, if you can't read that fast, you cannot learn. By some estimates, only one in ten second-graders at public schools in Latin America can pass the sixty-words-per-minute test. The other nine are heading for permanent academic failure. (Want to see the trauma of real second-graders trying to read and being unable to? There is a sobering video-documentary on Peru at https://www.youtube.com/watch?v=z-BQ_NFyeog.)

Remember, none of these services—birth certificates, nutrition, environmental stimuli, reading skills, and so on—is by itself sufficient. You need *all* of them. It is the combination that gives you a chance in life. And the timing of the combination is critical—there is a point beyond which the problem can be accommodated but not solved, no matter how much money you throw at it. Which brings us back to that baby in the Mozambican slum. Having no birth certificate may, after all, be the least of his problems. There will be plenty of hurdles that he will not be able to jump. You can safely bet that he will be one more case of wasted human opportunity. But it *surely* would have been nice to have a record of him—before he disappears in anonymity.

What do we know about informal workers?

In the average developing country, most people work outside the law—they have no contract, are not registered, carry no license, pay no tax, and make no pension contributions. They receive no social benefits or labor protection either. They are "informal." Think of the small farmer toiling on her tiny plot, the neighborhood's handyman working out of his toolbox, the lady cleaning houses for cash, the youngster peddling fake watches at the traffic light, the sweatshop operating in a basement, and the contractor that, literally, picks up day laborers on the street corner. These kinds of micro and small enterprises actually provide most of the world's employment. No wonder they have been the object of much attention by politicians, academics, multilaterals, NGOs, and virtually everyone else who has an interest in economic development.

Until very recently, our understanding of informality went more or less like this. To escape poverty, an individual starts a business. Happy with the initial results, she hires a helper or two. But soon she is faced with the government's taxmen, registrars, and inspectors. To her eyes, they want a piece of her income, in the form of taxes, fees, and bribes.

To hide from them, she keeps her trade minute, deals only in cash, and serves the kind of clients who don't ask for receipts. With those credentials, no bank wants to lend to her and no big company wants to train her as a supplier—she is cut off from both finance and technology. This forever condemns her to smallness, low productivity, and, very likely, poverty. The remedy? Lighten her tax burden, make registration and licensing painless, offer her basic training, and help her access "microcredit." For decades, this formula has been followed by policymakers and charities alike to usher people out of informality.

Well, over the past ten years or so, new data and new research have shown that reality is a lot more nuanced. To start with, evidence from Latin America suggests that a great deal of informality is voluntary—people are opting out of formality, rather than being excluded from it.[14] That may be because they don't value the benefits that the government gives them once they register. (If you barely earn enough to eat, how inclined would you be to make pension contributions? And what about contributions to the public health system, especially if public hospitals don't charge for their services?) Or they may think that the tax inspector is too incompetent to find them—"weak enforcement capacity," in economist jargon—or can be bribed easily if he does. Or the chances for expanding the business may be slim to start with—the client base may be as poor as the business owner. Or they may simply like the flexibility and independence of being their own boss. Whatever the reason, they *choose* to be informal, and the usual public policies and charitable programs can't really change that. Interestingly, in some Latin American countries (among them Brazil and Mexico), that choice seems to be related to age: the younger you are, the more likely it is that you will work informally for someone else (presumably, while you wait for a real job). On the other hand, as you grow older, chances rise that you quit your formal job to go solo and informal. Sounds sensible, doesn't it?

Second, the idea that informal firms are always less productive than formal ones has been proven wrong in, of all places, Africa. A 2012 study of nine hundred firms operating in three West African capitals detected large enterprises that dominate entire markets—say, grain imports—but operate as family businesses that meet few, if any, legal requirements.[15] (NB: just gathering so much enterprise information for that part of the world is a major achievement in itself.) It turns out that these "large informals" can be as productive as their law-abiding competitors. How so? One of an array of reasons is that big, informal entrepreneurs may find it easier to bribe their way to the top of the waiting list for public services—like electricity and water—which are essential to gain market share.

Third, credit is less of a problem for the informal sector than previously thought. True, banks rarely lend to people who cannot show proper books or titles to their properties—so the informal are still easy prey for loan sharks. But data from some twenty-six thousand South Asian firms hinted that, for those working outside the law, logistics can be more of a problem than finance.[16] In that region, things like electricity, transportation, and access to land top the wish list of those working informally—getting rid of crooked public officials comes in a close second.

Fourth, in some parts of the world (the Middle East is a case in point) informality may have less to do with economics than with politics.[17] The real dichotomy is not between formal and informal or big and small, but between "connected" and "not connected" to political power. What really matters is knowing the "right people." Those who lack connections tend to remain small and informal—in the periphery and "under the radar." Whether the recent wave of democratization—the Arab Springs—breaks that mold is yet to be seen.

Finally, informality is no longer considered a white-or-black phenomenon. Today, individuals and firms may abide by some laws and ignore others; they may pay taxes but skip on social security; have titles to their land but no operating license; they may have contracts for some workers but not for all. Even government-owned enterprises and institutions may qualify as "somewhat informal"— believe it or not, they are not always up to date on their pension contributions. Formality now has degrees; it has become a "continuum."

So, how will informality evolve over the next ten years? Nobody knows. But keep your eyes on three things: gender, aging, and technology. As more women enter the labor force, many of them will initially take the informal route, especially in developing countries. At the other end, as people live longer, they will retire from nine-to-five jobs to join the ranks of the self-employed, where they will be more likely to work in the shadows. And new technologies are already altering the value of size: while manufacturing is going for smaller, more efficient factories, dot-coms thrive in ever-expanding networks. There was no way Facebook could operate informally out of a college dorm for too long.

5

SECTORS

WHAT MINISTERS WILL WORRY ABOUT—OR SHOULD

Can governments create industries?

It is an old debate. Back in the 1950s and 1960s, from Asia to Latin America, an idea caught fire among development economists: governments should try to create industries. Typically, civil servants would pick industries that could employ lots of people or substitute imports, required huge upfront investments, were considered strategic, or just smacked of modernity. Those industries were then treated like "infants"—in need of all kinds of support until they could survive on their own. They were given tax breaks, protection from foreign competitors, cheap credit, subsidized energy, public contracts, even capital injections courtesy of the taxpayers. Think of toys, trucks, refrigerators, cement, steel, and petrochemicals—they were all going to be produced locally, whatever it took. (If you are over fifty and grew up in a developing country, fond memories of your family's car or TV set are surely coming to your mind: it carried a national brand, cost a fortune, and broke down all the time.)

The experiment ended in tears. Yes, there were a few successes in East Asia that astonished naysayers. (Legend has it that one of the world's leading banks told Japan in the 1960s that it would never be competitive at making cars.) But in most cases, the infants failed to grow and dragged the economy down with them. Consumers were saddled with lower quality products at higher prices, banks with unpaid loans, and governments with covering the losses of uncompetitive companies, year after year. Corruption added an ugly veneer to the whole thing—after all, you were giving away benefits to a chosen few. By the late 1980s, countries were busy selling off their public enterprises, opening their economies, and letting markets decide what was produced where. That, we thought, would be the last we would hear about "industrial policy."

Well, you'd be surprised. Today, developing countries rich in oil, gas, or minerals are desperately looking for policies to diversify their economies, not just because the price of natural resources could unexpectedly tank, but also because the business of extraction does not create enough jobs. They have money to invest—think Africa. Even in countries that are doing well, governments are searching for ways to make their industries more high-tech and avoid being trapped halfway up the technological ladder—think Brazil.[1] But everyone wants a new—read, smarter—industrial policy, one that avoids the mistakes of the past. They just might be onto something.

To start with, new industrial policy is not about bureaucrats picking products to manufacture domestically. If anything, it is about the private sector pointing out to policymakers the obstacles that make it unable to sell abroad—from a flickering electricity supply to corrupt customs officials. Far from closing the economy, the goal is to join the global market. Enterprises remain private. Everyone in the industry can compete for public support; it is not a privilege given to a favored firm or businessman. When public money is involved, it is mainly to improve logistics, infrastructure, or technology. Obviously, regulations that restrict trade are done away with first. A good example: a $10-million-a-year public investment in controlling skin parasites in cattle could unlock Ethiopia's potential as a major exporter of quality leather, assuming the virtual ban on leather exports was lifted.[2]

In fact, the new approach is really about information and coordination. If a public agency knows something that can help businesses prosper—say, a better technique to get organic certifications—it passes it along for free. If some regulation or procedure hurts investors—say, customs clearances that take too long—they have a friendly ear in a ministry to fix it quickly. The corrective actions usually call for coordination among many parties: it is not practical for hundreds of producers by themselves to try to negotiate free trade agreements, build ports, or draft laws. Instead, the government takes the lead on those initiatives. Of course, all this assumes that private business and public officials get along, share an objective, and have a system in place to communicate. And it is almost impossible when the basics to operate an industry—from a stable currency to respect for property rights—are not in place. That's why industrial policy, new or old, no matter how well intentioned, doesn't work when the rest of your economic policy is in shambles.

But how about new products? Who decides what *else* to export? There are some mathematical calculations that technocrats can make to sniff for markets where their country could do well, where it has "comparative advantage." (To get a sense of what comparative advantage means, ask yourself this: If you mow the grass much better than your gardener but are also an attorney making a thousand dollars an hour, would you ever touch the lawn mower? Lawyering is your comparative advantage.) But, in general, it is better to let businesspeople do what they do best: to find opportunities to make money. You can help a bit by, for example, letting them locate close to each other—in what are called "clusters." In Silicon Valley, Guadalajara, or Seoul, creative people feed on each other. Still, don't expect that totally out-of-the-blue products will always emerge; more likely, your industries will branch out gradually into ventures where they can use some of the knowledge they already have—from shoes to handbags, not satellites.

So, will this "new industrial policy," which sounds less exciting and less revolutionary than its previous version, work? Let's say that it cannot hurt. If done in the open, private–public collaboration is a win-win. But you are entitled to be skeptical, especially if your government has not been able to deliver simpler services—like a teacher in every class, clean water, and a decent police force. That is, if you live almost anywhere in the developing world.

Does foreign investment help you join global value chains?

When a respectable multinational company announces a new project in a poor country, it is usually a cause for celebration—especially when the project won't hurt the environment and won't corrupt public officials. These companies create jobs, pay taxes, and bring in badly needed foreign currency. More subtly, they also import better technologies, spread their knowledge, and hire local firms to supply them. This, one hopes, makes everyone more productive, even those that have little or no contact with the newcomers. Think of an international clothing brand coming to your town to set up a factory and export top-end apparel, or a mining giant breaking ground near your village to mine for copper and sell it abroad. They

generate benefits that go beyond their own businesses—
in technical jargon, they generate "spillovers" for the rest
of the economy. So, sensible governments do their best to
attract foreign direct investment. But, what evidence do
we have that these spillovers really exist?

A 2014 book edited by Thomas Farole and Deborah
Winkler uses a database of some twenty-five thousand
firms from seventy-eight developing countries to answer
that question.[3] What they found is quite surprising: for the
average developing country, in the short term spillovers
exist but are mostly negative! Local firms that are not
linked to the new foreign investment tend to suffer because
they find themselves competing for scarce resources like
skilled workers and electricity connections. It is only
over time—two years or more—that the entry of foreign
investors begins to benefit those who do not deal with them
directly. Typical case: Workers, especially young workers,
train according to the standards demanded by the foreign
employers but become available to local industries too.

Of course, not all foreign investment is the same as far
as positive spillovers are concerned. Mining shows fewer
of them than agribusiness. Joint ventures between foreigners and local entrepreneurs unleash greater and faster spillovers than projects paid and run only by foreigners. So do
projects that involve investors from neighboring countries
(they probably know the receiving country better) and those
who seek to create new markets (they are filling a vacuum).
Predictably, countries with larger technological gaps or populations with less education have a harder time extracting
spillovers from the foreign investment they pull in.

This last point hints at the hard truth: what kind of impact
foreign investment has on the overall economy ultimately
depends on how good or bad your general business environment is. Things like low inflation, open trade, sufficient
infrastructure, trainable workers, accessible finance, smart

regulation, secure property rights, and a government that treats investors fairly are all associated not just with more investment but also with more spillovers. This explains why foreign investments in Chile's mining, Vietnam's agriculture, and Mauritius's apparel have helped raise the productivity of workers and firms that operate outside those sectors.

It gets more interesting. Today, most foreign investment is linked to something called a "global value chain." This is the idea that most of the products that consumers buy—say, cars—are made up of parts and designs produced in different countries and shipped across borders to a final assembly site. (NB: now you know why speaking of an "American-," "Japanese," or "Italian-made car" is no longer that meaningful.) Yet, you can't be part of a production chain if you can't keep up with it. Imagine if your country manufactures the cars' tires, but because of poor port maintenance or unexpected changes in rules at customs, you can't be trusted to deliver the tires on time. Everyone else's effort along the chain would be wasted. How long before they cut you off? Why would you be invited in the first place?

You see, value chains force countries to rise up to a more-or-less common standard of efficiency. This is the real benefit of foreign investment. But it is also a warning: foreign investors will put their money into your economy and invite you into their value chains only if your country can offer two conditions. First, there must be enough local suppliers that can handle huge orders and can meet precise technical specifications—that is, enough large- and medium-size enterprises. These are not that common in the developing world, so economists advise latching to the section of the chain, where it is technologically less challenging, and then "climbing" from there. Second, because these days foreign investment is so closely associated with exports, it tends to go where the government is sold on the merits of international trade, facilitates—or, at least, does not hamper—the flow of goods across frontiers, and frees honest businesspeople to do honest business. In other words, when they decide whether to commit their capital, foreign and local investors think alike.

Can you innovate your way out of the middle-income trap?

It is one of those unproven but probably true facts that developing countries have an easier time getting out of poverty than getting into prosperity. They go from "low-" to "middle-income" level relatively fast but rarely make it to "high-income" status. (A country is considered middle income if its average citizen makes between twelve hundred and twelve thousand dollars a year, give or take a few dollars.) Somehow, they get stuck in a dreaded middle-income trap.[4] For them, the typical development story goes like this. They gain an initial boost by reforming their agriculture practices or by exploiting their oil and mineral reserves. This releases the labor and money needed to build industries that can use basic technology to cheaply produce the kind of goods that consumers in rich countries want to buy. Think of Brazil, China, Indonesia, Mexico, Russia, South Africa, or Turkey— chances are that your T-shirt, toolbox, teapot, and TV set were manufactured or assembled in a middle-income country like these. But when those countries try to climb up the technological ladder, sell more valuable stuff, be more productive, and create better paying jobs, things get complicated. Then the game is no longer to sell *cheap* but to sell *new*, not just to be *efficient* but to be *innovative*.

Economists more or less agree on what a country has to do to be efficient—open the economy, keep inflation low, treat investors fairly, regulate smartly, spend on education, build good infrastructure, and so on. But when it comes to making a country more innovative, the playbook is thin. You may hear words like "matching grants," "industrial clusters," "patent protection," "venture capital," and "incubators"—all techniques to put creative people together and give them the cash to do new things or to do old things in better ways. This is where your mind is suddenly filled with images of whiz kids trying cool ideas and becoming zillionaires. How on earth can governments promote that!?

A 2013 book called *Mass Flourishing*, written by Edmund Phelps, says governments can't.[5] Or, rather, it says they need cultural change. (Disclaimer: when this book was presented in Washington, DC, in the fall of 2013, I chaired the event.) Being innovative is in a society's DNA—or it isn't. Either we have an appetite for innovation—in his words, we are "modern"—or we don't—we are "traditionalists." Either our people are for intrinsic, imaginative, individual self-expression, or they are not. Either they want to live "the good life," or they don't. This is not only or mainly about bright scientists in a lab or rich businessmen in a factory. This is also about the poor, the uneducated, and the daring, ordinary folk bent on changing the world for the heck of it—a "mass flourishing" that makes countries more productive and, eventually, richer.

I know what you are thinking. Hold that thought. Mr. Phelps is not your average economist. He won the Nobel Prize—and just about every other prize the profession has to offer. You can't really get a PhD in economics without reading his mind-freeing papers. So, how does someone that credible come to the conclusion that innovation is rooted in culture? Simple: he looks at history. That is, the whole of history. His book is actually a review of the human experience from Jericho in 7500 BC to the White House today. Every civilization, event, leader, philosopher, technology, economist, war, army, thinker, city, inventor, banker, politician, crook, saint, empire, government, corporation, religion, painting, musician, and even movie director that mattered to history is named and placed in a chronological chain of events. Everything and everyone is in there, aligned, explained, and dimensioned. (NB: the World Bank and the IMF get one mention each.)

And sure enough, when looking at the grand tableau of history, Professor Phelps finds only a few places where "mass flourishing" and real prosperity ever happened: Britain, France, Germany, and the United States at various points between about 1820 and 1960. Thereafter, it has all been downhill. Even today, for all the might of the Internet, genetics, and satellites, he does not see a culture that nurtures innovation. But, wait, what about Steve Jobs? A one in a billion character. Twitter? Just a trendy way to conform. Silicon Valley? A rat race within the system. Fracking? A desperate technique in the hands of an old industry. Bitcoins? Funny money existed many times before. Megacorporations? They only care about their mutual-fund shareholders. China? More of the same, just cheaper. And so it goes. When compared with history, our inventiveness is in decline. We no longer live in societies where breaking the mold is the norm for *most* people—the "mass" in "mass flourishing." We are too dependent on government, community, and tradition. Collectively, we are not modern enough, in the right sense of the word.

All of this is, of course, impossible to prove beyond reasonable doubt. We simply don't have enough data. But it begs the question: If cultures are so important for the creative spark behind economic development, can they be changed through public policy? Can governments do anything to make their people more innovative? And if they cannot, are we saying that those middle-income countries that fail to climb the technological ladder are "trapped" *forever*? These are difficult questions. As it happens, we may be one step closer to answering them.

A team led by Dr. Jason Rentfrow of Cambridge University managed to measure an entire nation's distribution of personality traits across an entire nation—its "noncognitive skills."[6] That nation is the United States, no less. The team measured things like people's openness to new ideas, how conscientious they are in what they do, how they relate to others, and how stable their emotions are. Lo and behold, they found major differences across regions and states within the United States—yes, as it turns out, Californians *are* pretty innovative. A similar effort for developing countries is underway at the World Bank. (Another disclaimer: this writer is a regular commentator in that effort.)

Presumably, one day soon we will be able not just to know who is more creative—across countries, regions, generations, backgrounds, and so on—but also what effect, if any, government policies and programs have on our capacity to create. From public education campaigns, to tax breaks for inventors, to cheap credit for start-ups, we may discover that our attitudes can be changed. Think about it: Forty years ago, did we know or care much about the environment? It took a long time and lots of communication, but most of us finally came around to the idea that polluting is bad and recycling is good. Our cultural values do change. Maybe the key to the mass innovation needed for material progress is still within us waiting to be liberated.

From Miami to Mumbai: What makes cities competitive?

It is every mayor's dream to govern a city where businesses thrive, jobs are abundant, and people are happy. So mayors spend long hours trying to attract investors and please citizens. It is a tough job. They know they compete with other cities, both at home and abroad. They have zero control over crucial factors—like federal taxes or migration. And they know that there is no blueprint to guide them—they work mostly by trial and error. Lucky for them, this last bit of angst may soon taper off.

In a two-year-long effort, a team from the World Bank has painstakingly studied the performance of the world's largest 750 cities over, roughly, the past decade. Their report, aptly called *Competitive Cities*, was published in 2015, and it is quite an eye-opener.[7] What do cities that succeed have in common? What have they done right? And what do they still need to do to stay on top?

First things first. Of those 750 cities, only 130 managed to grow faster—in income, employment, *and* productivity—than the countries in which they are located. In other words, success is rare. When it happens, it can happen both in places you are familiar with—say, Dallas, Texas—and others you never heard of—do you know where Bucaramanga, Coimbatore, and Onitsha are? Among the cities that made it, you will find bustling marketplaces surrounded by rural areas, factory towns in industrial heartlands, and rich service centers booming in finance and tourism. There is no obvious pattern.

But, behind their wide diversity, well-performing cities have much in common. To start with, they had plans that built on their core strengths—if your brand was white beaches, you sought out nature-conscious hoteliers rather than car manufacturers. Those plans were seldom the brainchild of an enlightened leader but rather the outcome of consultation and partnership with both citizens and businesspeople. And they were kept flexible, learning and adjusting as they were put in place. (Speaking of core strengths and flexibility, you can follow a nail-biting, real-life case of how local development plans can fly or flop: in the next year or so, the city of Miami Beach will decide whether to save one of its last, most precious, beachfront parks—Allison Park—or give it away for ninety-nine years to a handpicked charity to construct its headquarters.[8])

In each of these successful cities, once the plan was agreed on, four main tools were used to implement it: reasonable institutions enforcing business-friendly regulations, accessible land serviced by good infrastructure, plenty of labor with the right skills, and support systems that ranged from market intelligence to workforce training. Mixed among those tools were subsidies. Yes, city governments usually lured firms with gifts—from tax credits to credit guarantees. How necessary those gifts were—and are—is a matter of debate. But one thing is clear: they worked better when they were given transparently and competitively—for all to see and for anyone to apply.

As much as they were the key ingredients, smart design and competent implementation would not by themselves have gotten the job done. What closed the circle of success boils down to one thing: leadership. Behind every city that flourished, there were leaders ready to bet their political careers. They convened, challenged, cajoled, and convinced others to move in a single direction—and to stay the course. They were the spark and the glue of their towns. Some of them came about as the result of matured political systems, and some were lucky accidents of history—something that puts a question mark on their replicability.

Now, how sustainable is the success of a city? After all, many mighty metropolises saw decades of glory, only to be followed by bankruptcy—think Detroit. Truth be told, cities are notoriously unstable arrangements—fiscally, socially, environmentally, and technologically. On the fiscal front, mayors have a burning incentive to overborrow. They can see themselves as merely "in transit" or "in training" for national-level office. Their tendency is to borrow as much as possible, cut as many ribbons as possible, and let their successors deal with the pile-up of debt. To make matters worse, lenders expect central governments to bail out big cities in trouble—"too urban to fail"—so loans are always on offer.

At the same time, competitive cities are expensive cities. The poor have a hard time living there and are pushed out to, or kept at, the periphery. Many are forced to squat in the outskirts in what, over time, become cities in their own right. And most rely on government—national or municipal—to pay for urban services like transportation, electricity, or water connections. Put differently, the transition to competitiveness needs to be managed if it is to be socially inclusive.

You can feel a similar tension between a city's economic success and its environmental sustainability. By some estimates, cities are responsible for more than 70 percent of the world's energy consumption and energy-related greenhouse gas emissions—a proportion bound to increase with population and income. They will also be prime victims of climate change—the rise in sea levels could sink many coastal cities off the map. In fact, one-third of those 130 successful cities sit by the ocean.

And then there is technological progress. To economists, the purpose of a city is "agglomeration"—humans come out with newer, better, and cheaper products when they are literally closer to each other. But the value of agglomeration is changing, perhaps undermined, by technologies like telecommuting, 3D printing, driverless cars, and remote-controlled delivery. Why do you need to be physically in the office to chat with your colleagues? Or keep large inventories in urban distribution centers? Or live downtown if you can sleep in a car that takes you there by itself?

We have no answers for those fundamental problems—at least yet. But there is no doubt that they will be easier to tackle in vibrant cities where people can prosper. On that, the lessons from around the world have shown the way forward. While still tough, the mayor's job has become slightly more doable.

How will technology shape the world of tomorrow's leaders?

Imagine you are invited to address an international gathering of young leaders—those brilliant, world-traveled, multilingual twenty-somethings who graduate from top schools with top honors and—having walked away from six-figure salaries—work for almost nothing in NGOs. Their driving force is the common good—that is, to improve the lives of people they don't know. Just by looking at them, you know that one day, one of them will be your president. Imagine also that they want you to tell them how the world will look when they take the driver's seat two or three decades from now. What would you say?

You surely don't want to start with, "When I was your age . . ." But you *will* think about it. Thirty years ago, the world was really very, very different. Technological progress has since changed everything—if you don't believe it try to picture life without the Internet. And our leaders have had to adjust to the consequences—both good and bad. What technologies could change us again in the next thirty years? What will these young leaders have to confront? Three guesses.

First, a limitless source of energy. Physicists may finally find a way to fuel us forever at zero or close-to-zero cost. (Don't laugh; they have been trying for a while to do just that through nuclear "fusion.") This would change all prices and our perceptions of what is valuable. All things manufactured would be cheaper. So would food, as would anything that needs to be transported or whose production can be mechanized. Poverty would fall, almost by definition. In fact, the definition of wealth would change too. What makes a nation "rich" would have to be reassessed.

Oil, gas, and coal would be as useful, and as valuable, as typewriters. In contrast, anything that is based on human intellect will be pricey. The *design* of blue jeans, computers, or cars—if we still use such antiques—will be more costly than their production. (We are not so far from that already, are we?) Lawyers, doctors, and architects would get even bigger salaries than the unskilled. Economists would call this a massive change in "relative prices"—the price of goods *relative* to the price of talent. In a world of endless energy, education would be king. Knowledge and ideas would matter much more than endowments and geography.

Second, a complete understanding of how the brain works. Think of the possibility of drastically expanding our capacity to think. Neurologists are far—but not *too* far—from opening the pathway into how exactly we process information, store memories, handle emotions, generate insights, and respond to stimuli. But say they can crack the "brain code"—sort of what Watson, Crick, and their successors did for DNA. This would put us in a world in which people's ability to understand, learn, communicate, and socialize could be easily scaled up—not just a bit, but manifold. This would bring the concept of education to a new level. Learning would be a fast, lifelong, and boundless process. Awesome mathematicians, critical thinkers, and polyglots would be the norm. School years (when you are educated) and years of schooling (for how long you are educated) would be all but meaningless. "Teacher" would be a relative concept. Workers would be more trainable and more productive. Professional qualifications based on degrees and diplomas would carry less weight. We would be able to say with scientific confidence that the new generations are indeed smarter. (If you think raising teenagers is difficult now, wait a few decades.)

Third, a ten-year increase in our life expectancy. This would mean that most people in developed countries—and most countries may by then be developed—would live into their nineties, especially women. Of course, life expectancy has risen before. But it took more than a hundred years for an average American male to live into his late seventies (in 1900, he would die in his mid-forties). Genetics might soon bring about a *sudden* jump in life's length across the board, for all countries and all sexes—say, by vanquishing cancer, AIDS, or hereditary diseases. Yes, the possibility of living longer will feel good for each of us individually, but it might cause huge collective problems. With most of us working into our seventies, where will the jobs come from? And, if we don't work longer, who will pay for our longer retirement? Not to mention the pressure on the planet's natural resources: with fewer people dying, the world's population would be permanently higher (until, that is, we decide to have fewer babies). We will consume more water, produce more trash, and make more trips. Political preferences will change too, hopefully for the better, if *older* humans mean, on average, *wiser* humans.

Now, to make it all the more exciting for your audience of young leaders, suggest to them that the three technological advances—limitless energy, formidable brainpower, longer life expectancy—may happen simultaneously. In the next three decades, physics, neurology, and genetics may deliver results that transform *who* we are and *what* we do. The new generation of leaders will have to deal not just with the benefits of that but also with the problems—technology can very well be used for harm. Life will not necessarily be easier, happier, or more peaceful in the new societies—it will just be fundamentally different.

All very futuristic, isn't it? Borderline fantasy? Well, imagine if in 1986, exactly thirty years ago, when most current presidents and prime ministers were "young leaders," you had addressed them in a conference with a speech like: "One day, all of us will be connected by inexpensive handheld devices that will, in the blink of an eye, carry messages across the globe, give us the power to search for and find virtually any information known to mind-kind, and guide us block-by-block through any city anywhere in the world. Trust me, you will lead a world of universal communication." It is difficult today to sense the respectful embarrassment that the audience would have felt with such an insanely sci-fi prediction. But technology proved it possible—almost easy. It is nothing compared with what will happen by 2046.

How will tomorrow's infrastructure be built?

In the old times—that's only twenty years ago—a federal minister of planning would sit in his office and single-handedly decide whether a road, port, or power plant would be built, as well as who would build it. Contracts would then be signed behind closed doors, bulldozers would roll in, and taxpayers would foot the bill—the entire bill. Well, those days are all but gone, and a new way of building infrastructure is taking shape.

First, ideology is being replaced by standards. Never-ending arguments about privatization—who should *own* the electricity company—have given way to public discussions about performance—who can avoid more blackouts. In fact, we now have standards of all kinds to compare the quality of infrastructure services across countries and even across cities.[9] Hours of uninterrupted water supply, days to get an electricity connection, cost of downloading a container, and kilometers of maintained roads, you name it, can all be measured. This makes it easy, politically and legally, to hire private companies to do the job—and to fire them if they don't. These "public–private partnerships" take many forms. Professional managers can run a state-owned water utility (as in Colombia, Gabon, and the Philippines). The government may guarantee a minimum income to a toll-road "concession" built by private investors (Chile, Mexico, India). Or a foreign firm can build and operate an airport (Greece, Jordan, Russia). The possibilities are virtually endless. In fact, if a standard of service can be articulated in a contract, the service can almost surely be delivered by a public–private partnership.

Second, as private investors join in, taxpayers are getting a break. The cost of roads, trains, and airports can be shifted more toward the *users*—whoever drives, rides, or flies pays a tariff for it. This could not come at a better time. Governments around the word, especially in rich countries, are too entangled in fiscal austerity to even think about paying for new infrastructure by themselves. Yes, there is China, with its trademark appetite for big projects. But even there, questions about fiscal sustainability are being raised. And there is, of course, the matter of generational fairness: if we make *today's* users pay, we don't have to saddle our children—that is, *tomorrow's* taxpayers—with so much public debt.

Third, infrastructure is no longer seen as a good tool for social policy. The idea that the government can help the poor by forcing utility companies to provide service at prices that do not cover cost has proven to be absurd. It is not only that the companies soon need to be bailed out with taxpayers' money, or that their managers give up on quality and customer service. The real reason is that most of the value of the subsidy is captured by the rich—after all, who consumes the most electricity, water, and gas? There are much better ways to assist people in need, directly and individually, without messing up the finances of your infrastructure suppliers.

Fourth, accountability is giving infrastructure a better brand. The image of the reckless multinational company bribing public officials, paving through rain forests, dumping chemical waste, and razing villages is becoming a thing of the past—not that it doesn't still happen, but it is a lot less frequent. Today, no serious corporation wants to be caught on YouTube corrupting, destroying, polluting, or usurping—if you don't believe it, ask shareholders at British Petroleum. In fact, private investors are beginning to embrace "safeguards," that is, practices that keep them honest, green, and socially responsible—Peru's mining industry has invested in some of the most environmentally friendly technologies that exist. This is good for business. And the safeguards themselves are much better and clearer than they used to be—right down to the number of trees you need to plant for every tree you cut down.

Fifth, states, municipalities, cities, and even communities, have a bigger say. As democracy spreads and urbanization speeds, local authorities are given more responsibilities—and more resources. They are receiving a larger share of national tax revenues and of the rents coming from natural wealth like oil or minerals. That "fiscal decentralization" gives them power, including the power to borrow. So they don't just run the local schools; they are in charge of services like water, electricity, gas, and transportation. They can build infrastructure by themselves. And they can block or delay any project that the federal government may plan in their territories—think of those angry neighbors opposing the expansion of Heathrow Airport.

Finally, developing countries are linking infrastructure with extractive industries. While commodity prices are no longer sky-high, and are likely to stay like that for a while, the appetite for exploration and exploitation of natural resources remains strong. And the amounts at stake remain truly transformative—enough to turn places like Ghana, Guinea, and Uganda into middle-income countries. So governments negotiate package deals that mix extraction rights with construction obligations—"You get access to our bauxite only if you build a port to ship it out that other industries can also use." Chinese companies are doing this all across Africa.

So, building tomorrow's infrastructure will be a collective effort: it will involve central governments, private investors, users, and local officials. Even extractive industries will be part of it. But will this mean more and better service? Not sure. What *is* sure, however, is that the previous top-down system is not coming back. And anyhow, it wasn't that perfect in the first place.

How green should economic growth be?

First dilemma. When your country sells its oil, copper, or timber, it is actually swapping one asset for another: out goes a natural resource, in comes cash. Your national wealth has not changed. Now, if the cash is invested wisely, you might be better off—rather than leaving hydrocarbons, minerals, or trees sitting idle, you would have healthier children, more educated workers, better infrastructure, and so on. But does that mean that you should drill, mine, or cut down as much and as soon as possible?

Second dilemma. An investor is about to build a huge clothing factory that will employ thousands of poor people in an otherwise hopeless town where unemployment and decay have been rampant for years. The factory will generate well-paying jobs, badly needed tax revenues, and—if things go well—a shot at attracting other investors. There is a catch, though: the factory's runoff will slowly but surely pollute the local river. In thirty years, its water will be foul and unusable. But that's thirty years away, and people are suffering now.

Would you join a demonstration to stop the construction of the new factory?

Third dilemma. A populous developing country finds a way to quickly grow its economy. Its billion citizens begin to demand condos, cars, refrigerators, and steaks. Producing all this for them will add tons of carbon dioxide to the world's atmosphere, an atmosphere that is already too warm because citizens in rich countries have been buying condos, cars, refrigerators, and steaks for decades. In the end, the warming of the global climate will hurt everyone—think catastrophic coastal floods, terrible droughts, and devastating storms. Should international organizations somehow try to persuade that developing country to slow down the pace of its economic growth?

Fourth dilemma. A hydropower dam could solve, once and for all, your country's perennial lack of electricity and unleash its industrial potential. This will surely be good for the environment because there will be less need to burn coal. Engineers are happy with the project's safety standards, and bankers are lined up to finance it. But just when the bulldozers are about to move in, someone finds out that the dam's reservoir will submerge the habitat of a particular type of squirrel that cannot survive anywhere else. That species will be gone forever. What do you do?

Final dilemma. Your economy depends heavily on oil imported from faraway countries whose politics are less than stable. The oil is then used to fuel cars whose emissions ruin the air. A local entrepreneur suddenly invents a new technology to extract gas from underground rocks. The procedure sounds brutal: you drill down deep and then blast the rocks with high-pressure water and chemicals. Out comes a lot of gas that can replace the dirty oil. But you are unsure what the long-term effects of that subterranean blasting will be. Contaminated groundwater? Leaks? Earthquakes? Even the name of the excavation technique—"fracking"—sounds a bit scary. Do you shut it down and continue to burn foreign oil, or do you take the risk and try the new technology?

By now, you should be struggling with the economic, social, geopolitical, ecological, and technological content of those dilemmas. If so, welcome to the quest for "green growth," that is, for the right balance between material progress and environmental protection. There is much debate over where and how to strike that balance. The debate boils down to societal preferences and moral choices—so, of course, there is little agreement. The caricature of the heartless economist and the tree-hugging environmentalist shouting at each other comes to mind. But don't throw in your intellectual towel just yet. Well before one gets to extreme dilemmas, there is a lot that can be done—based on common sense—to make growth greener *without* making it slower. There are win-wins.

To start with, governments could reassess the subsidies they provide. The prices of gasoline, electricity, water, and even food are usually subsidized—this is true in many countries, developed and developing. Because people don't pay for the true cost of what they consume, they have less incentive to conserve—why would you unplug your chargers at night if the electricity bill is ridiculously cheap? These price subsidies are not just inefficient but also unfair: Who drives the biggest cars and lives in the biggest houses? Certainly not the poor. Still, by some estimates, the world spends about a *trillion* dollars a year on this kind of giveaway.

Industries could be much faster in adopting cleaner technologies that already exist. Why aren't they? Because they don't always have to pay for the environmental damage they cause. Sure, when a giant multinational company spills oil in the coastal waters of a rich country, it is held accountable. But, in the day-to-day of business, there is plenty of pollution for which nobody pays. Think of the carbon emissions coming from the hundreds of thousands of airplanes and ships that carry the world's trade. But think also of the millions of subsistence farmers putting down one more round of pesticides, no matter how much they may hurt the environment, to squeeze a larger crop out of their tiny plot of land.

And consumers—meaning us—could change the way we behave and what we value. Whether we do laundry too much or recycle too little, these individual decisions are the result of the prices we face, the knowledge we have, and the social norms we follow. Who wants to drive a massive SUV if gasoline costs a fortune, you are aware of the car's crass carbon "footprint," and your friends would think it is uncool? The same applies to our appetite for "intergenerational equity," that is, for saving part of our natural resources for our children and their children. Is this really a priority for you, as a voter, when you have to pick one presidential candidate over another?

So, how does one get governments, industries, and people to do the right thing and go for greener growth? Surprisingly, the technical tools are known: undistorted prices, clear property rights, smart taxes, enforced regulation, markets in emission rights, community engagement, investment in research, finance for innovation, open data, public education campaigns, and so on. But, as with so many things in development, politics—and the power of those who benefit from the status quo—gets in the way of action, and reforms either don't happen or take a long time. And don't forget that, to be effective, many of those reforms need countries to act together, which adds a daunting layer of complexity. That's why, in the coming years, all eyes will be on emerging economies, on whether they will lock themselves in the old ways of doing business or will seek to grow *greenly* from the beginning.

Is it time to end fuel subsidies?

Every year, governments in the developing world spend half a *trillion* dollars making energy cheaper for their citizens—they subsidize the consumption of oil, natural gas, coal, and other fossil fuels. This is bad for social equity, for economic growth, and for the environment. But they do it anyway—a kind of fiscal aberration that has lasted for decades.

What's wrong with using taxpayers' money to make energy more affordable for everyone? The first problem is that not "everyone" benefits equally. In the average developing country, *two-thirds* of gasoline subsidies go to the rich—they have the cars—and only 3 percent goes to the poor—they rely on public transportation, where it exists. Something similar happens with electricity and natural gas—who owns the larger houses? These gifts to the well-off come at the expense of more and better services to people in need: a typical oil-importing nation could easily double its budget for public healthcare if it did away with fuel subsidies. Not that the amount of driving, lighting, or heating done by the rich would change much if they had to pay the full cost of the energy they consume—they are just happy to pay less and pocket the difference. It is difficult to imagine a more regressive way to spend public funds.

This points to the second problem with fuel subsidies: they are not very effective at spurring economic growth. Governments in oil-exporting developing countries lose, on average, the equivalent of 3 percent of GDP in those subsidies. But research suggests that a dollar spent on public infrastructure or on cash transfers to the poor generates more private investment and consumption than a dollar spent subsidizing gasoline or electricity.[10] In other words, letting the price of energy reflect its cost would generate large fiscal savings (aka "fiscal space"), which could then be used to stimulate the economy—an attractive proposition at a time when other tools, like record-low interest rates, have proven insufficient.

And, of course, making fossil fuels artificially cheap is a sure—and shameful—way to accelerate the degradation of our natural environment. Think of climate change and rising sea levels, and think of local traffic and air pollution: they all worsen when prices at the pump are kept artificially low. The International Energy Agency estimates that removing subsidies to the consumption of fuel would, by 2020, cut carbon-dioxide emissions by 7 percent—roughly the same as the current emissions of the entire European Union.

So, if fuel subsidies are that bad, why haven't they been dismantled already? Because raising prices is never popular and can lead to major social unrest—as Nigerians found out in early 2012. But, with sound planning, lots of communication, and a mechanism to compensate the poor, it can be done—as Indonesia, Iran, Malaysia, and Morocco, among others, have shown. In fact, the time has never been better to do it. The fall in international oil prices since mid-2014—from over one hundred dollars per barrel to around fifty dollars per barrel—has made it possible to reach a new social contract on fuel prices. Consider this: if your government was a year ago selling oil products at half their international value—not an unusual case—ending the subsidy today would imply almost no increase in price for the consumer. The key is to do it openly and prepare public opinion for the days when oil prices rise again—something that most macroeconomists expect before the end of the decade. When that happens, political pressure to go back to subsidization will mount. That is why this reform must be accompanied by programs to shield the poor from its impact. The good news is that, in most countries, those programs already exist and expanding them is far less expensive than fuel subsidies. Bottom line: We can build fairer, richer, and greener societies and still save money—a win-win-win opportunity that comes around once in a generation. We should seize it.

Can emerging economies have universal health coverage?

If you cannot pay for your daughter's polio vaccination, should the government pay for it? How about if she had cancer, and you cannot afford the treatment? And what if the terminally ill one was not your daughter but you? If you answered "yes" in any of those circumstances—and 99 percent of us would—you support "universal health coverage," that is, the idea that people should not be left to suffer, or to die, just because they are poor. What we usually debate—and vociferously so—is who exactly should be helped with taxpayers' money (only the poor? their children?), for what type of illnesses (contagious? complex?), and to what extent (full? partial?). These are ideologically supercharged questions. This is where conservatives' passion for personal responsibility rubs liberals' love for social solidarity. No wonder universal health coverage does not exist in the United States (where some call it "socialism") and is being cut back in Europe (where most call it "a human right"). But, while the debate rages in rich nations, successful developing countries like Brazil, Chile, China, India, and Indonesia have figured out a way forward and are moving ahead. Here is what they are doing.

First, they have reached a political consensus: if you cannot pay for healthcare, the government will pay for you. For them, this is not just moral principle. It is a way to ensure political stability. Which is worse for economic growth, to use public dollars to fund health services for millions in need, or to have those millions angrily demonstrating in the street? Solidarity is good for business. Of course, this assumes that you can tell who is poor and who is not. Well, now you can. Advances in biometric technology have made it easier and cheaper—less than four dollars per person—to identify individuals, to know their income, and to track what subsidies they are receiving. This may sound trivial if you live in Canada or in France, where you have an assigned social security number and "free" healthcare, courtesy of the state, from cradle to grave. But it is revolutionizing social policy in the developing world.

Second, publicly paid health coverage is being expanded beyond the traditional basic package—beyond things like vaccinations, maternal care, and family planning. As developing countries get richer, their pathological profiles change. Their people get sick from other things—diabetes, hypertension, cancer, and heart disease become more common. They also have fewer babies and live longer. So the old way of supplying healthcare needs to adapt. You spend more public money on teaching people how to live—eat less, exercise more, quit smoking, and use condoms. You train more doctors to be specialists rather than generalists. And you begin to worry about patents—can you afford the latest medicines produced by big-brand pharmaceutical companies, or should you challenge their intellectual property and produce a generic version of your own? Guess which way new global heavyweights like Brazil chose.

Third, while the government may be paying for health services, it is no longer the only provider. Building public hospitals and hiring doctors is becoming less important than making sure patients have health insurance and can use it to seek medical care from whomever they want. Many of the new providers are private—some for profit, some not. This allows governments to focus on, and do a better job in, areas where for-profit health enterprises do not want to go—say, remote rural villages. (For the record: When the government itself cannot extend these services, it is usually private nonprofit organizations that do the job—South Sudan, the newest country on earth, is a good example of that.)

Finally, as more private providers are paid with public money to supply healthcare, more emphasis is put on results and service quality. Has the incidence of malaria actually fallen? How many births were assisted by a doctor or a nurse? What percentage of young people contract sexually transmitted diseases? How long do patients wait for treatment? It is usually easier to hold a contractor accountable than a civil servant. And a contractor is usually more creative in finding ways to keep you from doing unhealthy things—Discovery Health, a private South African company, gives you "points" that you can redeem for discounts at the supermarket. No doubt the move toward universal coverage has brought about new metrics around health. But the real luck is that all this has coincided with an explosion of monitoring and evaluation techniques (M & E), which help us measure what governments achieve with every dollar they spend—the new generation of economists is obsessed with this.

So, how much will it all cost? Believe it or not, universal health coverage need not be expensive. Remember, it all starts with means-testing, that is, with spending more on those who can afford less. The average emerging economy already dedicates about 5 percent of its GDP to health; roughly half of that is paid for by taxpayers. And spending more does not ensure healthier citizens anyway—the United States has the largest health bill on the planet (15 percent of GDP), but for all its high-tech hospitals, it produces mediocre outcomes. Of course, cost is only half the equation—the benefit of living in a society where illness is not a sure path into bankruptcy, or death, must be worth something. The newly developed countries have understood that.

How do you measure the economic impact of Ebola?

The outbreak of Ebola in West Africa in 2014 claimed many lives—more than five thousand by some counts. It also had the power to wreck the economies of one of the poorest regions in the world. But, it didn't. The reason has to do with how people and governments behaved.

To put things in perspective, more than half of the twenty million people of Guinea, Liberia, and Sierra Leone live in poverty—real poverty. Their average annual incomes range from just over four hundred to less than seven hundred dollars. They have lived through violence and civil wars. But, in recent years, thanks to a mix of mineral discoveries and better governance, they were finally beginning to climb the development ladder. Ebola put all that into question. How bad was the initial economic impact, and how bad could it have gotten?

Answering those questions is more art than science. These countries were not flush with socioeconomic data to begin with. And there is much uncertainty about how far the virus, literally, travels. In a 2014 report, John Panzer, Francisco Ferreira, and their colleagues at the World Bank came up with some interesting estimates—and with an interesting way to estimate.[11] (Disclaimer: this writer was an adviser to their work.) They started by collecting information directly in the affected areas, from hotel occupancy rates and cement sales to farms that had been abandoned and mines that had been shut down. They added all this up and figured that, in 2014, the economies of the three countries drastically slowed down but did not contract. Their rates of economic growth were cut by about half. That is a loss of some $350 million—large for them, but not catastrophic.

Still, the sudden slowdown was more than enough to derail the finances of the three governments: they spent a lot more on health, while they collected a lot less in taxes—when a crisis of this sort strikes, paying taxes is at the bottom of a citizen's priorities. The fiscal hole was larger than what these countries spend on social assistance in normal times: from 2 percent of GDP in Guinea to almost 5 percent in Liberia. It was clear that they needed immediate help, about $400 million of it. Fortunately, the rest of the world was listening and money came in.

However, things could have gotten much more serious. To guess how serious, the World Bank team created an "Ebola Impact Index," based on air travel connections from and to West Africa, and on the quality of healthcare systems in countries to which West Africa is connected. It tells you roughly how likely it is that countries in Africa, Europe, and the United States be affected by Ebola. They then used some pretty sophisticated statistical tools to model the economic links between West Africa and the rest of the world. And finally, they built two "scenarios" for how governments and people might behave. The first scenario is one in which politicians—African or otherwise—act fast, in a coordinated and credible way, and contain the spread of the virus within a year—at twenty thousand cases, mind you. This makes people less afraid to leave their homes and return to work: trade, farming, construction, industrial production, even investment, all resume fairly quickly. The economy recovers, the total material loss for Guinea, Liberia, and Sierra Leone is "only" one hundred million dollars, and the rest of the world is spared the effects of Ebola.

But, what happens if politicians fail to act quickly, decisively, and together, and people panic? What happens if because the number of cases is allowed to rise to, say, two hundred thousand, workers, investors, traders, and farmers stay home? This is the second scenario—and it is sobering. Then the economic loss in the whole of West Africa, not just in the three initially affected countries, could climb to thirty-three billion dollars. That would be a devastating blow to the region. Rich countries like the United States, France, and Germany would still be spared, but the already wide wealth gap between them and Africa would grow even wider.

What makes all this very interesting is that the final economic toll of Ebola is not driven by the direct costs of the disease itself—expensive drugs, sick employees, and busy caregivers. It is driven by how much those who are *not* infected trust their governments. If public action is not seen as containing the outbreak and fear of contagion rages, workers will not go to work, business and factories will stay closed, and the economy will collapse. This is called "aversion behavior," a term you may want to keep in mind. Note that aversion is unrelated to the actual number of deaths a disease causes: *every year*, malaria kills twelve times more Guineans, Liberians, and Sierra Leoneans than Ebola has killed so far. But people behave differently in pandemics. We learned this with SARS in 2003 and with H1N1 in 2009.

A final point about social dynamics. Ebola knows no class. The rich and the poor can, and do, get infected and die. But for those who can afford prevention—from hand sanitizer to emigration—the chances of infection are much lower. In any scenario, the poor bear the brunt of this outbreak, not just because they are more likely to catch the virus but because they are more vulnerable to the economic impact of the disease. The prices they care about, especially of food, rise. They have no savings to rely on. And they have fewer transferable skills to look for safer jobs. If Ebola ever gets out of control, prepare to see more poverty in West Africa.

Is there new power in entertainment education?

Back in the mid-1970s, a soap opera did what no one thought possible—it convinced Mexicans to have fewer babies. Within a few months of the daily airing of *Acompáñame* (*Come Along with Me*, a privately produced, didactic story of three sisters who took very different approaches to family planning), Mexicans began to use contraceptives with gusto. Within five years, the rate of population growth slowed down by a full percentage point—a screeching halt by demographic standards. Of course, radio and television shows had been associated with changes in social behavior before (think of Britain's *The Archers*, a public-radio soap opera that was originally meant to help farmers raise their productivity after World War II, but has since brought the reality of rural life into the country's urban living rooms). But this was the first occasion that a *telenovela* was specifically designed to achieve a development objective *and* make money at the same time. "Entertainment education" was born. And an avalanche of replication followed—in India, in Kenya, in Tanzania, and in many other countries around the world.

Fast forward to 2016. Entertainment education has become a science. What was once a collection of experiments in public communication has become a powerful tool in public policy. What was meant to foster family planning has been scaled up to tackle some of the toughest problems in development—like gender biases, corruption, climate change, global diseases, and financial illiteracy. You can now target the attitudes that make us indifferent toward—or the culprit of—abused women, crooked politicians, polluting factories, malaria victims, or loan sharks. Call it "Entertainment Education 2.0." How did it happen? What changed?

First, technology has allowed for two-way communication. The good old radio and TV have been complemented—more than substituted—by computers, cell phones, and the Internet. Your audience can tell you in real time what impact (if any) you are having. Text messages, wall posts, and tweets provide instantaneous feedback—the "Like" or "Don't Like"—that you need to refine your message. Long, long gone are handwritten letters mailed by viewers through the local post office.

Second, we have a better understanding of how societies learn. They do so in steps: awareness ("A sex virus is going around") is followed by knowledge ("It's called HIV, and you catch it through unprotected sex"), then by a new attitude ("I'm worried about AIDS"), and finally by a new behavior ("We use condoms"). Attach those steps to a person that audiences can identify with (a role model), and you have a lesson in social conduct—and, possibly, a new cultural norm.

Third, competition in media has become much tougher. The market for entertainment is saturated. Viewers and listeners have hundreds of choices, even in poor countries. Screenwriters are constantly looking for an edge over their competitors. This has opened the doors of Hollywood, Bollywood, and Nollywood to NGOs and academics who can volunteer solid and ready-to-use information, rich in dramatic value. Who do you think provides the research when your favorite detective show tackles a serious issue?

Finally, the spread of democracy has turned development policy into a collective exercise. In the past, advocacy was mostly about convincing autocrats to do the right thing—to invest more in education, to avoid graft, or to respect minorities. Today, leaders—or most leaders—do what voters want. *People* have to be convinced. This has placed a premium on, and has raised enormous interest in, the levers to influence social values. And that's precisely what the new entertainment education offers.

Of course, there are risks. Who decides which values should be promoted? And how do we keep the techniques of entertainment education from being used for evil—like ethnic cleansing? Clearly, you need a framework of moral reference. Is it the United Nations Declaration of Human Rights? Is it a country's constitution? Religion? Tradition? These are important questions that may have no universally accepted answer. But, well before you get to these more difficult issues, there are plenty of practical problems that anyone, in any society, would agree to fix. Example: Holland recently used TV shows to alert youngsters to the damage that loud music can cause to their hearing—ironically, they listened.[12] Who can be against that?

Anyhow, we are far from having habit-breaking, sure-shot instruments to alter social behavior. We are far from "designer" cultures. And remember, this type of education only works if it entertains—meaning that it can turn a profit. But even if we can make *some* values change *somewhat*, it is still worth trying. Imagine if we felt half as passionately about our children's ability to read as we feel about our favorite football team's ability to win. Or if our knowledge about women rights equaled half of what we know about women celebrities. Or if we cared about our government's budget half as much as we care about our family's budget. You get the point. We always knew that societal preferences evolve—through the sudden emergence of an inspiring leader, a devastating crisis, or a transformative technology. But we couldn't quite *influence* the process. Now we can.

How do you deal with rising food prices?

For the poor, food inflation can be catastrophic. Imagine, when you live on $1.90 a day or less, chances are that you spend two-thirds of your income feeding your family.

More to the point, chances are that you do not save and already spend all you earn. When food gets expensive, you have to cut quantity, quality, or both. You eat once a day, not twice, or you buy cheaper staples with fewer nutrients. This can be devastating—not so much for you but for your children. Students cannot focus on learning when they are hungry, at any age. In other words, temporary spikes in food prices can cause a permanent loss of human capital. So governments, donors, and development professionals rightly worry about rising food costs. But panic is the enemy of sound policies. Rushing to intervene, politicians tend to ignore seven critical facts.

First, most developing countries are better off when food prices increase because they export more food than they import. For those lucky countries, better export values mean more resources to spend on education, health, and infrastructure. That is why they used to complain loudly when rich nations subsidized their own agricultural production and depressed international food prices for everyone (who can forget the fights during the Uruguay and Doha "rounds" of trade negotiations?). And that is why they will suffer much if global trade is interrupted. Think of Argentina, Côte d'Ivoire, and Thailand: Why should they wish the price of soybean, cocoa, or shrimp to fall, or want those markets to stop operating?

Second, not all of the poor are worse off when food prices rise. Those living in rural areas are likely to produce more food than they consume—in technical jargon, they are "net producers." For them, rising prices are a good thing. Not so for the urban poor (who are "net consumers"). It is in cities where the social impact of suddenly unaffordable meals is likely to be felt. Yet it is also in cities where it is easier to provide assistance (more on this below). Prepare to see villages prosper and slums suffer, and prepare to see less migration out of the countryside.

Third, helping farmers in the developing world become more productive is good for their incomes but does nothing to stop food inflation. More access to credit, know-how, and transportation can raise the yields and the profits of farming households. However, for most produce, prices are determined abroad; local production is just too small to make a difference. Yes, some perfectly nutritional crops are not demanded by foreigners (like Africa's moringa), so more domestic production may cool down their prices. But those crops rarely dominate the feeding menu—not to mention the preferences—of the poor.

Fourth, higher food prices in US dollars do not necessarily mean higher prices in the currencies of developing countries. A ton of oranges may sell on the international markets for a hundred dollars more than before. But it may simultaneously sell in Brazil for three hundred Brazilian reals less. The reason for this is that the real may appreciate against the US dollar. This appreciation has actually happened in many, if not most, emerging-market currencies. The dollar is not what it used to be.

Fifth, taxing exports does nothing to guard against food inflation. The tax just takes a portion of the higher price away from the farmer and gives it to the government. But the consumer still pays the higher price. How about banning food exports altogether? Would that help? Well, if you can enforce the ban—not a small "if"—local prices may fall. But the countries that usually purchase food from you will soon enough retaliate and stop buying your other exports too.

Sixth, central banks can do almost nothing to tame food inflation. There is no point in pressing them. Even if they raise interest rates sky-high, groceries will not become cheaper. Their price depends on what happens in the world, not in any one country. And anyway, most people do not buy food on credit.

Finally, price controls do not work. You may send the police to try to enforce them, but all you will get is empty shelves because nobody wants to sell at a loss. Hoarding, shortages, black markets, and a lot of corruption usually follow. For the poor, the problem is now double: food is not only expensive, but it is also difficult to find.

So, what should governments do? Keep their nerve, let markets work, and compensate the poor. Higher international prices will be passed to consumers, and part of national production may even be exported. Additional transfers of cash will be immediately needed for those who cannot fend for themselves, especially children. What if the logistics to make the transfers are not in place, or if we just don't know who is poor and who isn't? Then, instead of giving out cash, you should give out food—through meal programs in schools, work-for-food exchanges, or direct distribution centers. It may sound complicated, but the alternative is much worse.

What are "commodity super-cycles," and why do they matter?

The average developing country lives off exporting commodities like oil, gas, copper, cocoa, or soybeans. The sale of these resources brings both revenue to the government and foreign currency to import what is not produced at home—which, in these places, tends to be most things. So whatever happens to the price of those commodities matters a great deal for development and, even more, for the war on poverty. The problem is that those prices are famously volatile. They can jump up and down seemingly at random, from year to year, month to month, even within a single minute. This makes life miserable for those who have to plan public investments in schools, hospitals, or roads. Statisticians and investors have studied the problem at length, not least because there is a lot of money to be made if you can find a predictable pattern. And despite all their efforts, they have come up mostly empty-handed.

Mostly. There has always been suspicion that, if you took a really long view—we are talking centuries here—you might uncover periods of about forty years when commodity prices steadily climb for a decade or two, only to fall slowly back to where they were. That is, you might uncover "super-cycles." It may sound crazy but before anyone could actually find one, plenty of theories were put forward to explain why super-cycles happened and what to do about them. The stories went more or less like this: A technological innovation triggers a period of prosperity in a large, advanced country—after all, they have most of the scientists—and its industries and cities begin to demand more energy and food from abroad. Think of Britain's industrial revolution in the late 1700s sucking raw materials from the developing world, and you'll get the picture. Prices for coal, cotton, sugar, tea, and the like go up and greater quantities are produced. But over time, the innovation wears out, demand dwindles right when supply is growing, and the prices of commodities tumble. This is the end of the super-cycle.

Now, all this could have just been a topic of academic banter—fun but inconsequential. Except that it came with a dangerous recommendation to governments in poor countries: try to use the times of commodity bonanza to create local industries, at any cost, even if you have to use taxpayers' money. Otherwise, you will be left with nothing when the downturn comes. Many heeded the advice and followed this path, with disastrous results, from isolation to corruption to inflation. (If you are a Latin American over fifty, you probably suffered through this.) Remember, this advice was based on a phenomenon that we could not see! By the late 1980s, two Nobel-laureate economists (Gary

S. Becker and Paul A. Samuelson) had denounced super-cycles as, well, baloney.

Was it? In 2012, new research claimed to have found evidence of commodity super-cycles.[13] What's more, it suggested that we were then in the middle of one. The claim is based on two methodological breakthroughs. One is better and longer data. The other is a statistical technique called the "band-pass filter"—think of it as playing with your camera's zoom until you get a clear photo of your son's entire soccer team. Put the two together and it turns out that, over the last one hundred and fifty years, the world has been through three complete super-cycles, each about four decades long, and each making commodities between 20 and 40 percent more expensive, before prices dropped back to their previous levels. They all took place around major shocks to the global economy: World War I, Europe's reconstruction after World War II, and the Arab oil boycott of the early 1970s.

But the new findings shed light on other, more current questions. First, if we were in the upswing of another super-cycle until mid-2014, what was driving it? In a word: China. The new economic superpower's appetite for commodities had been raising their prices since the early 2000s. No surprise there.

Second, is there a very long-term decline in commodities? Except for oil, probably yes. Controlling for inflation, during each super-cycle the *average* price of commodities has gone down, in some cases by a lot—metals and agricultural products have fallen by about one-third and one-half, respectively, over the last century and a half. (Hard to believe, but back in the mid-1800s most commodities were much more expensive than today.) Oil, on the other hand, has tripled in value.

Third, are new technologies for exploration and exploitation increasing the speed at which we can find and extract oil, gas, and minerals? Yes. From airplane-mounted detectors to fracking, we no longer have to wait decades before supply responds to demand and larger quantities of commodities reach those who want to buy them. Ergo: when the next downturn comes, prices will fall faster than in the past.

Finally, and perhaps the most important question, should developing countries try to use their commodity income—while it lasts—to build industries? Surely diversification has huge benefits. You don't want to depend on one or two natural resources that generate few jobs. But that's true regardless of super-cycles. And it does not necessarily mean more factories and mass production, good as those may be. Different from the times of industrial revolutions, modern economies prosper on services and cutting-edge technology. The real trick is to translate the upswing of the cycle into human capital and knowledge.

How do oil-rich governments respond to falling oil prices?

Seasoned macroeconomists like to repeat a dogma they hold dear: governments should take positive shocks as temporary, and negative shocks as permanent. This way, you will not binge in good times or procrastinate in bad ones. Alas, few governments heed the advice. Take oil for instance. When its price booms, politicians in oil-rich countries rush to spend as if the bonanza will last forever. And when it tanks, they delay belt-tightening, hoping for a quick rebound in prices. You can't blame them—they tend to choose policy responses that are popular with voters. But, as we learned in 2014, some responses can be more damaging than others.

After four years hovering above a hundred dollars per barrel, oil prices collapsed in the second half of 2014. They have since fluctuated around fifty dollars per barrel, and the consensus forecast is that they will not recover their previous high levels in the medium term. The new reality hit oil-dependent countries hard—affecting their growth, exports, and fiscal revenues. After all, in the average oil-dependent emerging country, oil accounts for a fifth of GDP, half of fiscal revenues, and three-quarters of exports. That is, even small fluctuations in price have a major impact on economic performance.

And yet, in almost all cases, the initial reaction of policymakers was, well, no reaction at all. As fewer dollars were coming in, no immediate cuts were made to public expenditures, no taxes were raised, and foreign exchange reserves were used to defend the value of the local currency. In a mix of denial and delay, they wishfully expected prices to recover quickly. Why go through the pain of adjustment if things will return to normal in no time?

Within a year, it was clear that things were not returning to normal—the "super-cycle" in oil prices was over. So governments began to do their homework. What they did falls into three broad categories. First category: adjustment. Countries like Azerbaijan, Algeria, Kazakhstan, and Russia accepted that with fewer dollars flowing in, their currencies had to be devalued—by half or more. At the same time, these "adjusters" tried to offset the loss of fiscal revenue through higher tax rates—especially VAT—and cuts in subsidies—notably, those related to energy. Sales of public assets were sometimes part of the package. When necessary, local banks were helped—you don't want a banking crisis on top of an oil crisis. To keep inflation from spiraling out of control—with the devaluation, imported goods became more expensive—central banks were given more freedom to raise interest rates. And to cushion the social impact of the new austerity, some transferred cash directly to the poor and the elderly. If everything works out, the final result should be the return of economic growth, and some inflation.

Second category: partial adjustment. Some oil-exporting countries did not devalue their currencies, either by choice—say, Saudi Arabia—or because they don't have a currency to devalue—say, Ecuador, which uses the US dollar as its legal tender. That made the adjustment more painful. It involved deeper cuts in public investment, higher tax rates, the elimination of subsidies, privatization of state companies, the opening of the oil sector to private investors, and the search for new foreign creditors. If you were lucky enough to have put money away in a rainy-day fund during the boom years, this was the time to tap into it. (That is exactly what Saudi Arabia did with its half-trillion-dollar reserves). Otherwise, you faced a long period of recession, but no inflation.

And then there is the third category: no adjustment. These are countries that tried to ride the downturn in oil prices by imposing foreign exchange controls, that is, by requiring that all sales or purchases of foreign currency have a government agent as a counterpart, and this agent be the one to set the price. The controls usually included a ban on holding foreign currency, in cash or in banks, and on transferring it abroad. Governments were thus forced to ration their country's reserves of foreign cash: decide what imports would be paid for, oblige exporters to give up their earnings, and choose which external debt to service. To different degrees, Angola, Nigeria, and Venezuela followed this path.

For this third cohort, the results ranged from bad to disastrous. Trade was seriously disrupted. The rationing mechanisms initially focused on imported luxury items but soon affected imported production inputs—from fertilizers to spare parts. Later, shortages of essential imported goods developed, including basic food and medical supplies.

Domestic commerce and provisioning was interrupted or went underground. Hoarding and smuggling flourished.

Less formal trade meant less growth. But foreign exchange controls hurt growth in other ways too. They cut off local industry from global value chains, as it could no longer be trusted to deliver on time—an essential condition to be a member of a chain. Uncertainty over profit repatriation and debt repayment froze most forms of foreign direct investment and external credit. Corporate debts with foreign lenders went unpaid and defaults ensued. The domestic banking system faced a double whammy: depositors withdrew their cash—to try to exchange it for dollars—and borrowers stopped repaying their foreign-currency loans.

Sure enough, people found ways around the controls. An illegal, or "black," market for foreign currency developed. The gap between the value of the dollar in that market and its official value grew enormous—it reached over 1,000 percent in Venezuela in 2016. This pushed inflation to spiral—in the streets, the price of anything imported followed the exchange rate of the black market. Inflation was pumped up even further by the money printing necessary to fund the widening deficits in the unadjusted fiscal accounts.

The damage to the economy and to society went beyond dry macroeconomic indicators. Institutional quality crumbled, as an increasing number of public agencies were drafted into the administration of the rationing of foreign currency—the central bank, the tax agency, customs, even the police. At each control point, the probability of corruption grew exponentially. The distortion in prices reached absurd proportions—a prime example is Venezuela, where a gallon of gasoline was selling for less than ten *cents* (US). The final bill from not adjusting was a toxic mix of recession and inflation that, you guessed it, hit the poor hard.

So, after the initial denial ends, what is the real choice oil-rich countries face when the price of oil collapses? The choice is between adjusting with growth and inflation, or adjusting without growth and without inflation. This may be a bit of an oversimplification, and each country has its own peculiarities—some are more prudent than others during good times. What is clear is that not adjusting is not an option.

Should foreign aid be abandoned?

In his 2013 book, Angus Deaton, a Nobel laureate and an idol among development data junkies, made two claims.[14] First, advances in medicine have helped humans live longer and better lives. Over the centuries, greater awareness of germs, the discovery of vaccines, and the use of sanitation drastically brought child mortality down, initially among rich families in rich countries. Other people and other countries followed. More recently, progress was—and is being—made against the kind of chronic diseases that kill the old, like strokes and cancer. So, up until about 1800, you were really lucky if you lived past forty. Today, you are likely to clock seventy or more. We have managed to "escape" death—or, rather, to postpone it. But not everyone has escaped. Huge differences exist and persist *within* and *across* countries—by some estimates, poor American males die about five years earlier than their rich peers, but more than twenty years later than the poor in Nigeria.[15] Where you are born, and how rich your family is, can easily add or subtract a decade from your life horizon. Millions still die of preventable or curable diseases. Not what one likes to hear, but the facts are impossible to

disagree with. (Disclaimer: when Professor Deaton publicly—and brilliantly—presented his book in Washington,
DC, in December of 2013, this author was the commentator
on his presentation.)

It is the second claim in Professor Deaton's book that
makes you scratch your head. He says you cannot help
those who have not yet "escaped" by giving money to
their governments. To him, the "foreign aid" provided by
rich nations and multilateral banks to developing countries is almost useless, probably counterproductive, and
should be abandoned—all $120 billion a year of it. This is
not an unusual claim. Many see government-to-govern-
ment charity as a way to dominate former colonies, impose
models and values, subsidize the donors' contractors and
consultants, take care of security concerns, and prop dictators. To prove it, they only have to point to an inconvenient
truth: after fifty years and more than three *trillion* dollars in
aid, poverty is still alive and well. Why keep giving? And
money is fungible, anyway. When you donate to build a
health clinic, you may make it easier for politicians to buy
weapons—now that they don't have to pay for the clinic.

More damaging, aid is said to break the fundamental
contract on which every society rests: citizens pay taxes
and that gives them the right to demand services from
their government—like good schools, passable roads, and
an honest police force. Why would a politician tax his voters and be pestered by their resulting scrutiny if a nice, rich
country is willing to bankroll him? In technical parlance,
foreign aid weakens governance. Ergo: scrap foreign aid.
Or at least make sure you spend it on things that benefit the poor in general—not in any one country—such as
research on tropical diseases.

The problem with these arguments against aid is not
that they lack fiscal appeal or past evidence—nobody
wants to waste money abroad while the budget is being

cut at home. The problem is that they belong to a world that
doesn't exist anymore. Start with governments in developing
countries. They are no longer free to do anything
they please, even if a donor tried to force them to. They are
subject to tougher "accountability frameworks." Think of
these as four "D's"—democracy, decentralization, devices,
and debt. Politics has over the past decade become much
more contestable in most places. You are more likely than
ever to be kicked out of power—or face social unrest—if
you cannot deliver or if you are caught stealing. This is
not to say that incompetence and corruption do not happen.
They do. But it is becoming more difficult to get away
with it. This is not just about voting presidents in and out
of office every four or five years, or the opposition having
a voice in parliament. It is also about the local mayor
or governor, not some faraway federal minister, taking
responsibility for your children's schools or your city's
hospital—the "D" in decentralization. When public services
are bad, you can embarrass those leaders into action
in real time by texting, tweeting, or posting from your cell
phone—"D" for devices. And how about the big policies
that can make the economy thrive or tank? Who else keeps
an eye on that, apart from the IMF? Markets do. Even poor
African countries try to sell sovereign bonds—"D" for
debt—to foreign and domestic investors. You can't do that
if your economic policy is a mess and potential lenders
don't trust that you will pay them back. None of this is
waterproof, of course. But it makes the idea that foreign
aid relaxes pressure on the governments who receive it
sound a bit beyond the point—these days, the pressure
comes from elsewhere.

What about multilateral institutions like the World
Bank? Doesn't their aid weaken governance because it
replaces the need to tax? Well, for most developing countries,
money from multilaterals is not much larger than a

rounding error in the governments' financing plan. Many of these countries have gained access to finance on their own, and many get large revenues from the sale of oil, gas, and minerals. Think of the governments of Brazil, China, Colombia, India, Mexico, Russia, or South Africa. Their financial needs are giant compared with any foreign aid they might receive. In fact, they value aid as long as it helps them solve problems that they cannot solve by themselves—in other words, they value aid if it carries knowledge, not just cash.

Finally, and beyond becoming more accountable and relatively smaller, there is another tectonic plate that has been shifting underneath foreign aid. We—meaning, anyone with a stake in economic development—are on our way to knowing all the poor by name, one by one, individually. This started fifteen years ago in Mexico as a way of transferring cash to those in need. It soon became obvious that to make the transfer, the Mexican government had to meet the person, identify her, collect her basic data, and establish a logistical mechanism to pass on the cash—be it a kiosk, a debit card, or a cell phone. At last count, some seventy developing countries—thirty-five of them in Africa—have these kinds of transfer systems in place. At the same time, the cost and speed of biometric identification are collapsing—to less than four dollars and five minutes per person, as India has shown. This technology opens a logical crack in the main argument against foreign aid. If it is true that giving aid to governments weakens their resolve to serve their people, don't stop aid; instead, give it directly to the people. You now have the tools to do it. But is aid large enough to make a difference? Well, Nga Nguyen and this economist calculated how many African countries receive enough aid to lift all their citizens out of extreme poverty—assuming aid was individually distributed.[16] The answer is twenty-five. Not a bad start.

What's the future of foreign aid?

Rich countries have been giving money to poor ones for many decades and for many reasons—from geopolitics to postcolonial guilt to altruism. Much of that money was meant for development, that is, to build the schools, hospitals, and roads that, over time, would make the recipients less poor. This Official Development Assistance—that's what it's technically called—was sometimes sent directly and sometimes through multilateral organizations like the World Bank. It came as grants and as soft loans—so soft that many were later forgiven—and it was big: this economist's back-of-the-envelope calculation is that, over the past fifty years, net ODA has added up to about three and a half *trillion* dollars in 2011 prices. To give you an idea, that's about three times larger than the entire economy of sub-Saharan Africa. And the flow continues to this day, at about $120 billion per year.

You'd think that was good. What can be wrong with international philanthropy? Well, foreign aid has been criticized from lots of angles. It is said that it has propped up dictators who were happy to siphon the funds into their own accounts abroad. That it was self-serving, as only companies and consultants from the donor countries were awarded contracts. That it ignored local priorities and preferences, and literally bulldozed its way into communities. That it imposed economic "models" that clashed with local realities. That it was volatile, jumping from one flavor-of-the-month issue to the next without sticking long enough to make a difference in any. That it overwhelmed already weak civil services, which had to meet the peculiar administrative requirements of each donor. That it achieved very little, especially in lifting people out of poverty. That it created "aid dependency" because recipient countries did not bother to set up proper tax systems. The list goes on and on.

Much of that criticism is valid. But things have changed. Over the past decade, traditional donors have begun to demand political freedom or, at least, less political repression before they disburse. Since 2000, they have tried to track results, initially through the so-called Millennium Development Goals, a set of worthy commitments regarding extreme poverty, primary education, maternal health, and the like. In 2015, those commitments were upgraded to the Sustainable Development Goals, which the international community pledged to achieve by 2030.[17] Since 2005, donors have also made a genuine effort toward harmonizing their procedures and aligning behind the strategies of the recipients—rather than imposing policies from outside.[18] They have financed fewer construction projects and more policy reforms. They even wrote off massive amounts of debt, in exchange for promises of more social expenditures and less corruption. By early 2013, thirty-six countries had received some seventy-six billion dollars in debt relief.[19] And one can only guess that rich countries will continue to look for maximum impact from each aid dollar—after all, many of them face years of tough austerity at home.

However, the real change in—and the future of—development assistance is not coming from its traditional donors but from its recipients. First, some of the latter have developed enough to become donors themselves—think of the role that China, Brazil, and India now play in Africa. These newcomers have learned the lessons of the past, ditched the aid mentality, and see themselves more as partners than as donors. They are more interested in trading raw materials and investing in infrastructure than in exporting their own way of thinking.

Second, aid flows are being dwarfed by revenues from oil, gas, and minerals. Many, if not most, developing countries have plenty of money of their own, as they are discovering and exploiting natural resources at an unprecedented pace. Very few governments still depend on donations to pay teacher salaries or build power plants. Those who don't need the aid are disinclined to accept conditions or, even less, instructions from foreigners.

Third, today's average developing country has access to private funding. Some of it comes from investment banks that, apart from demanding good economic management, ask few questions—in larger countries, private loans dominate public-financing plans. Some comes from mega-philanthropists and their foundations—think of the progress the Bill and Melinda Gates Foundation has made in the fight against malaria. And some comes embedded in the work of dozens of NGOs and global funds that provide services for which, otherwise, the government would have to pay—say, for HIV/AIDs treatments.

So, if its recipients have cash and options, will official aid end? Probably not. No sensible government snubs an offer of free or cheap money. And places where the state is fragile or conflict rages need all the help they can get. The real question, though, is whether aid will remain *relevant*, and if so how. The answer boils down to this: solutions. Governments in developing countries will seek assistance only when they have a problem that they cannot solve by themselves. They know how to build schools, hospitals, or ports, and can pay for them. But they will look for other countries' experiences when reforming educational curricula, designing health insurance systems, or regulating private suppliers of infrastructure. They will want to avoid the mistakes of others and learn from their successes. At times, they may ask for support in implementing particularly tricky projects, mostly as a way to minimize graft, pollution, or resettlements. In other words, what will make future aid relevant will be knowledge, not dollars. And the donors that will be sought after, rather than just accepted, will be those who can deliver ideas, experiences, expertise, lessons, evidence, and data. Development aid will be a more difficult business—for you will need to operate at the technical cutting-edge—yet a more useful one.

6

AFRICA

THE LAST FRONTIER

Is Africa's emergence for real?

Do you sometimes wish you had bought property in Mumbai, Shanghai, or Rio ten years ago? You would have more than tripled your money. Well, ten years from now, you will regret not having bought in Abidjan, Dakar, or Nairobi today. Sub-Saharan Africa—"Africa," for short— is about to emerge. In the decade through 2015, Africa grew fast and continuously—its economy expanded at an annual rate of about 5 percent. This pace, which slowed down in 2016, was almost three times faster than the decade before.[1] Actually, the continent had never grown that quick for that long. It even breezed through the 2008– 2009 global crisis—it decelerated but did not shrink. Part of this was due to better policies, fewer wars, and, ironically, no financial sophistication. Much has to do with *China's* new presence in the region, with booming international prices for *commodities* until mid-2014, and with the viral spread of *communication* technology—that is, with the "three C's." But more profound and more powerful forces will, with a bit of luck, drive the continent's emergence. Here they are.

First, nobody knows how rich Africa actually is—how much oil, gas, minerals, and other resources lie beneath its surface. Less than half the continent has been geologically surveyed. It would take about one billion dollars to fly planes with magnetic anomaly detectors (MADs) to map it all out. Accounting for this resource wealth would change things. Countries that know for sure what they have can negotiate better extraction deals, get cheaper loans, and involve citizens in monitoring it all. Recent oil discoveries in Ghana are a good example of this.

Second, Africa has a lot to learn. There is a massive inventory of proven technologies that the region has not acquired, adopted, and adapted. Imagine, for example, what African agriculture would look like if it upgraded its production methods—like Brazil did forty years ago. Or if its transportation system were faster, cheaper, and safer. Or if it could harness more of its immense sources of energy. The technologies to do all that already exist. The good news is that the cost of transferring and protecting them is falling worldwide—Africa has yet to tap this knowledge.

Third, the region barely trades with itself. Only ten cents of every dollar exported from an average African country goes to another African country—in East Asia, half of every dollar exported is bound for an East Asian market. The opportunities for mutual benefit are huge. Energy is a good example. A few nations—among them the Democratic Republic of Congo—have enough hydropower potential to provide electricity to the whole continent. Yet, they do not. Another example is services: African countries do not readily recognize one another's teachers, doctors, or accountants, so professionals cannot move where they are most needed. And for all the images of malnourished children, Africa could feed itself if it allowed food to cross borders more easily—the travails of women carrying vegetable sacks on foot and trying to clear customs have been the subject of many infuriating reports. This self-isolation is slowly beginning to change—but agreements to form "regional economic communities" within Africa have existed for decades.

Fourth, Africans are joining the middle class (regional definition: those living on two to twenty dollars per day). By 2030, one in two of them—some six hundred million—will be middle class. Today, less than one in three is. This will change consumption habits—more TVs, cosmetics, and cars will be demanded. More importantly, it will also change politics. Radicals will be less welcome. Drastic change in policy will be less frequent. And planning horizons will be longer.

Fifth, Africa's population is maturing. This should bring a "demographic dividend," that is, every worker will have fewer children and fewer elderly to support. As the odds that your child survives improve, you limit the number of your offspring. In fact, infant mortality has fallen fairly dramatically over the past twenty years. So African women are actually having fewer babies—on average they still have more than five each, mind you. All this, of course, could be derailed by diseases like HIV/AIDS or malaria. And some countries, especially in West Africa, have yet to make progress in family planning. But the trend toward a more mature Africa is undeniable.

Sixth, agriculture will be transformed. The continent has some 200 million hectares of land that contain no forest, show good agro-ecological potential, house few people, and are reasonably close to a city. No other region can offer this. Yes, ownership of that land is in many cases unclear—titles, when they exist, are hotly disputed. But the combination of prices and possibilities will make the expansion of commercial-scale farming all but inevitable. Will this spell disaster for the poor smallholders that currently populate Africa's agriculture and provide most of the region's employment? No. If the links between big and small exist, both should be better off—Brazil and Thailand have shown that to be possible. But there will be fewer farming jobs, which takes us back to China.

Seventh, China will soon start outsourcing low-skill manufacturing jobs—perhaps as many as eighty-five million over the next ten years.[2] This will give Africa a once-in-a-lifetime opportunity to jump-start its industrial base. It stands a good chance of capturing some of that employment. It has a young and plentiful labor supply, and relative proximity to the United States and Europe (the main destination of Chinese products). This could not come at a better time—some 17 million jobs have to be created every year just to keep African unemployment from rising.

Eighth, over the next decade, there will be wholesale generational change among African leaders. A younger crop will come to power. This is not just about biology—although more than half the region's presidents are sixty-five or older. It is about the two-thirds of the population who are currently under the age of twenty-five, are more likely to be social-media connected, and are less likely to feel personally identified with the struggles of independence. The political discourse will change from past to future.

Ninth, whichever generation comes to power, it will be held to greater accountability than before. Democracy is—slowly—bringing voice and participation to African societies. As information and connectivity reach an ever-increasing number of voters, they will demand better service from their leaders. Decentralization of decision-making is already putting pressure on local authorities to perform. And Africans are beginning to use the tools for social accountability with gusto—from access to information laws in Uganda to cell-phone-based systems for reporting on absent teachers in Tanzania. All this will translate into better governance. Still far from optimal, but better.

Finally, there will be more peace—or at least less war. Many of the old African conflicts, whether over resources, race, or religion, are still unresolved. But prevention, attention, and intervention are more common—and faster. Look at the lessons of Côte d'Ivoire or the forward march of

Rwanda. If anything, the real worry is to see a small core of countries left behind, entangled in never-ending conflicts.

Put it all together and Africa's recent shine begins to look more permanent. Of course, many things can still go wrong, from a rich country's debt crisis pulling the global economy into a protracted depression to a permanent collapse in commodity prices triggered by a sudden cooldown of East Asian economies. But, if the world holds, this ought to be Africa's time. And it is for Africans to make the most of it.

Can Africa be defragmented?

The scene repeats itself daily. At a remote border crossing between two East African countries, a woman carrying an impossibly heavy load of eggs on her back is harassed—or worse—by custom officials. She arrived on foot, and the eggs are the produce from her meager farm miles away. Selling them in the neighboring country is her only chance at making a living. But either she pays the officials or she won't be let through. She pays—price: one egg. A few yards ahead, she is stopped again. And then again. By the time she gets to the market on the other side of the border, her load is forty eggs lighter. Her profit is all but gone. Since there is no other way—literally—to reach her clients, she will go through this all over again in a few weeks. Funny, these two countries belong to a "customs union," a treaty that has supposedly made commerce between them seamless and duty-free. Welcome to the mind-boggling cobweb of obstacles that make Africa unable to trade with itself. (By the way, if you are interested, there is a superb video documentary where you can hear this and other similar stories told by the actual victims; you can find it at https://vimeo.com/32976732.)

Now multiply the scene by hundreds of thousands of poor farmers across hundreds of thousands of miles of borders and you will understand why Africa routinely fails to feed its people. "Food-surplus" countries just can't send their excess to "food-deficit" ones. And what is true for grains, vegetables, and meats is also true for engineers, doctors, and nurses. The trade in professional services—in fact, any service—faces the same type of "nontariff" barriers, a code word for the dozens of bureaucratic permits that make it impossible to enter a market. Ask yourself why Ghanaian accountants—who are said to be pretty good and in large supply—cannot work in other West African countries that are short on bookkeepers. Or why there are so many unemployed teachers in Kenya while, just to its south, Tanzania has a shortage of them. How about trucking licenses that are not valid once you cross a frontier? Or telephone and banking services? Wherever you look, African markets are fragmented, that is, you cannot move your products from one market to another. The end result is that Africa has integrated with the rest of the world—mostly selling commodities like oil, minerals, or cocoa—faster than with itself.

The unfortunate thing is that fragmentation is costing the region billions of dollars and millions of jobs. At a time when the traditional markets of Europe and North America are stagnating, blocking intra-Africa trade seems like a self-inflicted wound. It aborts the type of global value chains that helped make East Asia the powerhouse it is—a final product is assembled from intermediate parts that are manufactured wherever it is cheapest. It makes it more difficult to diversify Africa's export base beyond commodities. And it is plainly unfair: it keeps the poor, especially poor women, from earning a living in activities where they have an advantage—like catering for smaller, local markets across the border.

How do you fix this? A 2012 book makes a strong case that the solution is not about presidential summits where free trade agreements between countries are signed—good as those may be.[3] It is not even about changing laws and regulations within each country—although some of those may need changing. The real question is about vested interests, something economists elegantly call "political economy." How come institutions, like customs agencies, that are ordered to keep trade flowing free just don't—or even do the opposite? Whom are they protecting? Who protects *them*? That's the real question. And it has no easy answers.

There is hope, though. Multinational action is beginning to bear fruit. Mutual recognition of some certifications is allowing a trickle of professionals to try their luck abroad but within Africa—if you travel the continent enough, you soon learn to recognize those brave South African agronomists helping raise crop yields in faraway farms. And each time famine strikes in one area, the light of enraged public opinion is shed over the inventories of food sitting idle in another. (NB: nothing promotes intra-regional food trade faster than charities and development agencies buying their food donations for Africa within Africa.)

But what will really drive change is that Africans are getting tired of this self-imposed isolation—wouldn't you, if, say, a bag of cement in your country cost three times more than in the country next door, just because your government wants to protect a local cement company and its private owner? Sure, trade within Africa won't become truly free overnight. It took Europe some fifty years to come together as a "single market." And, with forty-eight nation-states south of the Sahara, there will always be a few that refuse to join economic hands. As democracy takes hold, however, more and louder voices will be heard against internal barriers. In the end, those ladies with the eggs on their backs will carry the day.

Can Africans become shareholders in their own wealth?

Almost twenty years ago, Mexico did something that, until then, only rich countries had dared to do—it began to transfer cash directly to its poor. The payments were conditional: the recipients had to help themselves by keeping their children in school and vaccinating them. Today, some seventy developing countries have followed the example, and most evaluations show that the idea worked. But direct cash transfers can be more than a smart way to deliver social assistance. In fact, they may provide Africa with a neat solution to its most urgent problem: how to handle its massive commodity wealth.

Vast discoveries of oil, gas, and minerals—and, until mid-2014, high prices for those commodities—are turning the continent into a giant boomtown. Big money has been flowing into governments' coffers. The risk that it may be wasted—or stolen—is big. The best way to hedge that risk is to upgrade public institutions like budget, investment, and anticorruption offices. But that will take time. What can be done in the meantime? Transfer part of the money directly to the people—universally and uniformly, same sum to each person, rich or poor. Call them "direct dividend transfers."

Why would you do that? Will this not mean less money for schools, clinics, and roads? Not necessarily. In fact, direct dividend transfers may lead to less poverty, less corruption, less waste, *and* more public services. First, take poverty. If a typical African government (think Gabon's) distributed, say, one-tenth of its hydrocarbon or mineral revenues, each one of its citizens could receive about $100 per year. That may not be much for the well-off; they may

not even bother to collect it. But it would be a huge help
for poor households—a day-and-night difference in their
efforts to climb out of poverty. And if you are not just poor
but also female, the transfer would carry a welcome dose
of personal independence as well. Optimally, one would
like to focus the transfer only on the poor and away from
the rich. But, in most places, that would prove politically
complicated, if not impossible. And anyway, the rich are
very few. (If you are interested in this, in a 2014 paper, Nga
Nguyen and this writer calculated how much that 10 percent distribution would mean for citizens in each African
country.)

Second, direct dividend transfers would lead to less corruption. The best way to understand why is with a hypo-
thetical. Say that you get home tonight and your spouse is
waiting for you with a surprise gift—a brand-new Ferrari.
That will probably make you very happy. But you will soon
ask yourself: "Where did the money come from? I didn't
know we had that kind of cash." The same will happen
to people if their government all of a sudden gives them,
say, 10 percent of its mineral revenue—they will want to
know what the government is doing with the other 90 percent! You will create a "scrutiny effect," a popular interest
in how the bureaucracy manages the national treasury. In
technical parlance, you will have fostered the "demand for
good governance." (By the way, if you were getting a cut
of the profit from your country's gas industry, would you
insist on its nationalization or on its efficiency? Would you
want it run by politically appointed public employees or
by profit-driven private managers?)

Third, there would be less waste. Governments in
resource-rich countries are always under political pressure
to be seen as passing some of the dividends to the population. The usual means have been to give tax breaks, sell
fuel or food below their cost, or give away jobs in the civil

service. All this has in practice been captured by the rich and the connected. (Rule of thumb: the average developing country spends more on subsidizing public college education for the rich than on primary schools for the poor.) If anything, giving people a direct stake in their country's riches can be an opportunity for—and can be funded by— the abolition of other inefficient, inequitable, and morally questionable transfers. You get a dividend, but you accept to pay full price for what you consume. Iran has used something similar to dismantle subsidies for gasoline.

Fourth, there would be more public services. A big argument against direct dividend transfers is that they would leave less money for the government to invest in "public goods"—things like primary education, basic healthcare, and crime prevention. Point taken. But whether that happens depends on how much revenue the government is *already* receiving. If your country is so poor that the state is unable to provide much in terms of services (think of newly independent South Sudan), you may not want to take money away from it. But how about countries where the government has for decades appropriated *all* the revenues from commodities—billions upon billions of dollars—and has, by and large, wasted them? Will sharing part of those revenues with people reduce the quantity of public services or will it reduce waste? Look at most hydrocarbon-rich economies, and you will find the answer.

More subtly, direct dividend transfers could help national unity. In countries where regional, racial, or religious differences make it difficult to agree on how to share natural wealth—a problem that is all too common in Africa—the idea that everyone gets a cut of the riches, personally and individually, regardless of location, skin color, or faith, just for being a citizen of the country, may be a useful source of national identity. (Yes, new biometric tools can take care of misidentification and fraud.)

So, adapting Mexico-style social transfers to Africa's dividend transfers could work in theory. But, can it work in practice? After all, Africa is not Alaska, where oil dividends have been distributed to residents since the early 1980s. Well, the necessary technology is getting better and cheaper by the day—it costs less than four dollars to biometrically identify someone. And with the viral growth in the use of magnetic cards and cellular telephony across the developing world, making payments is a nonissue. More to the point, some thirty-five African countries already operate more than a hundred cash-transfer programs as part of their social policy. It is now a question of automatically and explicitly linking those transfers to the source of income from which they are paid and extending them to all. Of course, sitting governments have little or no incentive to do that—they would lose the power to decide who gets how much. More likely, direct dividend transfers will be championed by opposition politicians in contestable democracies ("Vote for me, and the oil is yours!"). In other words, the time is coming—in Africa and elsewhere.

How have the world's newest nations fared?

How do you start a country? Say that your province or region suddenly becomes an independent country—with recognition from the United Nations and all. After the celebrations end and the celebrities leave, the real decision-making begins. Will you have your own currency? What kind of taxes will you impose? What services will the government provide and to whom? Will you keep your borders open to people, goods, and money? If you happen to be rich in natural resources, who will exploit them and how will you share the income? And what about building state institutions like the police, the courts, and the central bank?

These questions are far from academic. More than thirty countries were created in the past quarter century alone. Think of Namibia, Lithuania, Georgia, the Czech Republic, Eritrea, East Timor, and Kosovo. And think of the newest nation on earth—South Sudan, born in July 2011. For none of them has nationhood been easy and, truth be told, few have so far succeeded. What are the lessons? Successful new nations have done a handful of things right from the beginning.

First, they quickly agreed on how to fund their new governments—and kept them from running large deficits. This is no technicality or accident. It usually implied tough decisions over how to share tax burdens and revenues from commodities—Kazakhstan is an example of the latter. Will the oil that happens to be in one area be used to benefit the new country as a whole? How about taxes that are bound to fall on one group more than another? If foreign countries make donations, how do you tell them—politely—that they cannot tell you what to do? And, wherever the money comes from, how do you make sure that it is spent wisely rather than disappearing through corruption? You see, the initial legitimacy of a new state hangs on its capacity to manage its fiscal affairs.

Second, they visibly delivered a modicum of public services. Remember, many of these countries arose from years of war and from larger countries that broke up and separated. Their infrastructures, schools, and hospitals were dilapidated, damaged, or destroyed. So simple achievements like reconnecting street lighting, paving roads, or restarting classes brought an early sense of progress—and of a functional government in charge. Ironically, it was not always the government who delivered the services; in many cases, it was private charities.

Third, they had currencies that people trusted. Some created their own new money (Namibia introduced the

Namibian dollar). Others adopted someone else's (East Timor opted for the US dollar). But the new countries that did well avoided inflation—let alone hyperinflation. Stable prices are in themselves a sign of an economy returning to normalcy. And they make it possible to build a banking system where, with luck, households can safeguard their savings, businesses can get credit, and everyone can make payments.

Fourth, they got their economy restarted. When the turmoil of national birth is over, people need to go back to work. Finding them jobs is not easy—especially when fighting has been the sole occupation for much of your labor force. There are typically two sources of immediate employment: reconstruction and agriculture. Just clearing out roads and helping small farmers venture back to their fields can put a lot of people to work. But it is not enough. The key is to lure private investors, local and foreign, by signaling that you will treat them fairly. Remember, you have all the appeal but also all the risk of a "frontier market." If you don't pass the laws (say, a companies bill) and build the public institutions (say, a bankruptcy court) that businesspeople need to operate, you can't expect them to bet their capital in your new country. This is less cold-hearted than it sounds. Usually, many of the early investors are members of your own diaspora. They may be morally identified—and excited—with nationhood, but they will still need a minimum of reassurance.

Finally, successful new nations stayed open. For them, independence did not mean isolation but integration. Many of the countries that sprang out of the former Soviet Union ran to join the European Union. Others sought new friends in—and banked on the goodwill of—the international community. New countries rarely had large industrial bases, so they had to import much of what they consumed. And anyway they could barely control their borders—migrants and commerce flowed more or less unimpeded. So, in practice, they learned to live with globalization from the start.

Is that all? Certainly not. There are plenty of other things to do—protecting people and their property, settling border disputes, demobilizing fighters, managing expectations, creating a sense of national identity, all while leaving no social or ethnic group behind. But those are tasks that become even more difficult if the initial economic policies are wrong—or missing. Future new countries should take note of that.

Can Africa compete with China?

It is accepted wisdom among economists that no country can out compete China—it will always be cheaper, faster, and tougher than any other. No matter how technologically sophisticated a country's industries are, when their Chinese peers enter the market, they can out price, out speed, and out live anyone. If that's the case, Africa has a big problem. Its hope of selling something aside from oil, gas, and minerals—something that creates enough jobs—lies in the type of low-skilled manufacturing where China rules. Game over? Not quite.

Africans have lots of opportunities to trade that they have not yet exploited—opportunities outside China's reach. The first of these low-hanging fruits is food. The continent has not yet commercialized its agriculture—it has not linked its small, subsistence farmers with the kind of corporations that can bring equipment, technology, and infrastructure. When that happens, China would likely be a buyer of African food, not a competitor. Sadly, today those farmers find it difficult to sell their produce across borders even *within* Africa, mostly because of excessive bureaucracy and corruption. The grand pan-African market is so fragmented that, in practice, it barely exists.

Second, even at their low-income levels, African consumers are very specific in their preferences. Take clothing, for instance. Yes, mass-produced, Chinese-made T-shirts and blue jeans are unbeatably cheap. But how do you explain that, in West Africa, the market for wax-print fabrics—those beautiful, shiny colors worn by African women and men on special occasions—is still led by a company (UNIWAX) operating out of Côte d'Ivoire and not by mass-producing counterfeiters in East Asia? Answer: African designers are quicker to capture the constantly changing local fashion. That sort of commercial niche, built on a combination of knowledge and speed, is still in its infancy, but it will grow apace as more Africans join the middle class. (As noted, depending on how you count, by 2030, one in two of them—about six hundred million—will be middle class.)

Third, international trade need not be only about goods—it's also about services. Of course, Africa's natural beauty makes it a unique tourist destination, one that remains grossly underdeveloped. But so is the often overlooked trade in professional services. African accountants, doctors, nurses, teachers, and others are locked within their countries' own borders—their degrees and certifications are rarely recognized elsewhere in the region. These same kinds of restrictions apply to banking, trucking, and logistics. This is a self-inflicted wound—you can't blame China for it.

Fourth, simply put, only Africans can convincingly produce African art. This is not about touristy souvenirs—many of those are actually made in China. This is about Africa's fast-growing multimedia. Who had heard of "Nollywood"—Nigeria's burgeoning film industry—twenty years ago? Today, it is said to employ two hundred thousand people, turn out twenty films a week, and is the third-largest movie industry in the world.[4] This success is not necessarily due to cinematographic quality; rather, it comes from the unique African-ness of the product. Something similar is happening in music. And the continent is only now connecting to the Internet and its possibilities—at viral speed. All this exportable art is yet to be supported by serious enforcement of intellectual property rights. But it is a sign of the times that a new African business line is the potential victim, not the perpetrator, of intellectual property violations.

Finally, and perhaps most important, wages and land prices in Africa are still very low, while in China they are rising by the day. (A good example: industrial wages in Ethiopia are a quarter of China's.) Yes, the productivity of African workers is an issue—they lack training and equipment. And, yes, land in Africa is not backed by good infrastructure, especially roads. But a 2012 study shows that, with better policies, more investment, and a bit of luck, many African economies could soon be globally competitive in "light manufacturing," things like footwear, furniture, and low-skill metalwork.[5] The claim sounds credible. After all, most African products can enter the United States and Europe duty free and quota free—China's can't. And it would really be a pity if Africa did not seize its wage and land advantages to enter the market for light manufacturing, not least because China is about to exit it—by some estimates, the East Asian giant will eliminate eighty-five million jobs in that sector over the coming decade.[6]

So, in the fierce competition of international trade, a competition that China has learned to master, does Africa stand a chance? Yes, it does. Not that it will be easy or quick. Some countries will do what it takes to compete, while others may remain stuck in exporting only natural resources. The good news is that the opportunities are there for the taking.

Can Africa follow China's industrialization path?

The simple answer is no. But there is a lot that sub-Saharan Africa (again, Africa for short) can learn from the Chinese industrialization experience—the incredible transformation from an old, inward-looking, heavy industrial sector that provided relatively little employment, exported nearly nothing, and was owned and managed by the state, into the world's most formidable light-manufacturing machine, run by private entrepreneurs and home to hundreds of millions of jobs. In two decades, the country's share of global manufacturing exports rose from nearly zero to 15 percent—to a third if you only count labor-intensive products. Here are the main lessons African policymakers can draw from this.

First, China's march toward factories actually started in its farms. In the late 1970s, rural households were given the freedom to manage the land they worked on. They were not given ownership of the land, just the power to decide what to do with it. This raised their productivity and income, eventually allowing many of them to move to cities in a flow of labor that kept wages very low for thirty-plus years. Africa is far from that. Its agriculture is still dominated by subsistence farming. Yes, it has a large and youthful population. But no African country can offer a supply of workers of the same magnitude, quality, or mobility that China had.

Second, China integrated itself globally, regionally, and subnationally. The driver of industrialization was the relentless pursuit of exports. That required not just cheap prices but also borders open to imported inputs, foreign investment, new technologies, and knowledge of what other societies like and want to buy. It also called for fluid trade with countries in the immediate Southeast Asian neighborhood, to form value chains (in which, as mentioned, final products are assembled with components manufactured wherever the cost is lowest). And, of course, within China, people, capital, and ideas went wherever new export industries demanded them—primarily to the coastal areas. This kind of multidimensional integration of trade corridors does not exist in Africa. The region has succeeded at globalization—selling commodities to other regions—but it has failed at "continentalization," that is, at letting goods and services flow from one African country to another. It remains a highly fragmented place, even in basic industries like food. This is due to a combination of misregulation, monopolies, and corruption. The result is that only 10 percent of an average African country's exports travel to another African country; the equivalent number in southeastern Asia is more like 50 percent. In other words, Africa must first defragment if it wants to industrialize.

Third, the Chinese government became an unwavering promoter of export-oriented private investment. Political leaders, both central and local, made it their job—actually competed—to attract new industrial projects. They removed logistical obstacles. They formed joint ventures. They built industrial parks, zones, and clusters. They even mortgaged public land to get bank loans and used them to build better infrastructure for business. (It doesn't hurt that Chinese households save almost half their income and deposit most of it in banks.) Not every project was effective, profitable, or easy to administer transparently. But the single-mindedness of it became a magnet for private investors. Few African countries today can show that kind of strategic clarity. Even fewer have achieved a level of government decentralization where local officials have the power, the means, or the institutional capacity to lead development policy. Devolution remains a pending agenda.

Fourth, China did not rely on massive natural resources. Economic growth was earned the hard way—farm by farm, factory by factory, and shop by shop. There was no oil, gas, or mineral bonanza pumping billions of dollars into the economy and into the government's coffers. If anything, China had to import natural resources. This should make industrialization relatively easier for Africa, a region super-rich in commodities. But it depends on how that wealth is spent. Is it going to build Africa's human capital? A more reliable electricity supply? Better roads? Faster ports? A more efficient civil service? While progress is slowly being made, the jury is still out.

Finally, China's industrialization also carries lessons for Africa about what not to do. Letting local officials, rather than markets, decide which firm gets land or a phone line or water service, and which one doesn't, may not be the best or cleanest way for Africa to allocate inputs. The continent already has plenty of experience in this and, by and large, it has not been a happy one—think of fertilizer-distribution programs. Setting up and managing a giant network of public enterprises, some owned centrally and some locally, some in full and some in part, some collectively and some individually, some with private investors and some not, may be beyond the institutional capacity of the average African government. And channeling people's bank deposits into public industrial ventures may deter Africans from saving more, which they need to do.

But, why is all this important for Africa now? Outside South Africa, isn't the region's industrial base puny anyway? Less than 5 percent of its GDP? Well, a 2012 book by Hinh T. Dinh and his colleagues at the World Bank argued that Africa should prepare to capture some of the lower tech, light-manufacturing industries—and jobs—that China will be shedding over the next decade.[7] These are things such as clothing, shoes, food, and furniture. As mentioned, by some estimates, there may be around eighty-five million jobs for the taking. Even if many of these jobs end up staying in South and East Asia, it is still a great opportunity to jump-start Africa's industry. At the very least, it could help focus the attention of African leaders and usher them to remove the many bottlenecks in their countries' industrialization paths (the "marginal binding constraints," in technical speak). Dinh et al.'s book masterfully lists those bottlenecks, not in theory, but by chronicling the life of actual Chinese enterprises, comparing that to what their African peers go through, and urging African politicians to do something about it. That would be good, for if there is a message in China's industrial success, it is this: there are no shortcuts.

Can services drive Africa's development?

The conventional map of Africa's development path went more or less like this: Transfers of capital and technology would ease people out of farming and into factory jobs around cities, while income from the extraction of oil, gas, and minerals would help governments pay for education, healthcare, and infrastructure. At the end of it, most workers would manufacture goods that the world would want to buy—at salaries that workers in richer parts of the world would shun. The problem with this march toward "industrialization" is that it has not happened. Africans did move, and are still moving, into cities. But once there, they are stuck producing services, not goods, mostly informally. The talk is of "premature deindustrialization."[8] Not even the prospect of China shedding millions of low-skill manufacturing jobs has changed that.

There are, of course, many reasons why Africa has not yet industrialized on a large scale, for example, poor governance and bad logistics. It will take decades to fix those. So, the question is, can services be the next engine of economic growth for the continent? Can Africans export enough services to each other and to the world? There is no data to answer these questions with precision. But Nora Dihel and her team at the World Bank had a brilliant try at it. They went directly to the source. Through thousands of old-fashioned, face-to-face interviews and some cool new methodologies—like crowdsourcing and "mystery shopping"—they amassed a wealth of information on African service providers. They talked to street vendors, hairdressers, housecleaners, doctors, nurses, teachers, bankers, accountants, lawyers, and just about everyone else making a living in the service sector. And they did it across all sub-Saharan Africa. What they found, presented in their 2016 book, challenges deep-rooted preconceptions.[9]

The first surprise is that virtually all services can be—and are—traded among and beyond African countries—even the most seemingly menial. Sure, local barbers stay local. But Tanzanian Maasai hair braiders travel to Zambia where their skills are in high demand—they have a brand on what they do. Sometimes, it is service companies that open branches in another country—South African banks come to mind. Other times, it is the consumer of the service who travels—think tourism. And, increasingly, it is the product of the service that is digitally shipped abroad, like a draft tax return prepared in Zambia for a South African client. The level of technical sophistication ranges widely; there are housekeepers and there are software designers.

Trade in African services is not just varied—it is also huge and booming. Much of it goes unrecorded—more on this later—so it is difficult to come up with a dollar estimate. But interviews with cross-border service providers—from gardeners to programmers—suggest that these are well-paying jobs that are lifting and keeping people out of poverty. They also suggest that providing services to or in another country is a great way for females and the young to make a better living. The fact that most respondents see their trade as a long-term occupation speaks for itself.

To Africans' credit, all this trade happens *in spite of* a cobweb of laws, regulations, and policies put up over the years by their governments, ironically, to protect national sectors and professions from foreign competition. In many countries, getting a work permit approved, a university degree recognized, or a branch licensed is virtually impossible for a foreigner. So plumbers, doctors, and insurers have to work informally or recruit local partners. Inevitably, corruption pops up and bribes are paid—those Maasai hair braiders can tell you a story or two about how expensive crossing a border can be. Add to that the problem of cooperation: you need coordinated action on both sides of the frontier, and that rarely happens. The result is much less trade in service, fewer jobs, and more poverty. Africa's recorded exports of services is a mere 2 percent of the world's total. This shows both that much of it happens under the radar of official statistics and how big the potential for doing more is.

In fairness, African leaders have in recent years tried to remove the barriers that hinder trade in services. They have signed plenty of regional agreements to make things easier. Two trading blocs—the East African Community and the Common Market for Eastern and Southern Africa—have shown the way. But laws and regulations are one thing, another is practice. Actual traders report little change in how tough it is to conduct business across countries. (NB: to motivate change on the ground quickly, in their book, Dihel and her colleagues advocate a pan-African "Charter of Traders Rights," a kind of public promise by all governments in the region that, in essence, would say: "If you come to any of our borders, we won't stall you, rob you, or harass you." That could work, if monitored by civil society organizations.)

All this has, of course, a not-so-rosy side. Exporting services sometimes means exporting your best and most dynamic people—those you need to build your country. Yes, they send remittances back home. But the "brain-drain" is large and painful. By some calculations, one-quarter of doctors trained in Africa eventually migrate to developed countries. Something similar probably happens to nurses, architects, and academics. But blocking their way out with legislation and bureaucracy is a self-defeating proposition—it just pushes migrants underground and leaves them unprotected abroad.

So, with all its pros and cons, is trade in services the future engine of Africa's development? Probably not *the* engine, but one of them, and one that can power others—agriculture, industry, and natural-resource extraction will do better if cross-border services do better. Remember: when you import a service, you are importing knowledge, and that makes you more productive. If the engineers in your neighboring country are better than yours at running the electrical grid, or its businesses use better processes, why not learn from them? The beauty is that, for all its recent vigor, trade in services remains an unexploited source of economic growth, and policymakers have the key to tap into it. They just need a bit of leadership and a lot of coordination.

Can Africa feed Africa?

Africa does not produce all the food it needs. In fact, as more Africans leave their rural villages and move to cities, more maize, rice, wheat, and other staples have to be shipped in from outside the continent. The cost is huge—well above twenty billion dollars per year—and demand is projected to double by 2020. Yet politicians tend to worry about this only during times of crisis, when the all-too-frequent drought or war unleashes those uncomfortable images in the media of sick children with bloated stomachs and hungry adults begging behind distribution trucks. By then, there is no alternative but to bring even more food from abroad. But why is Africa so food insecure? Doesn't it have some 400 million hectares of agricultural land waiting to be cultivated?

A 2012 report shows that the problem is mainly man-made—you can't really blame fate or nature.[10] It has to do with laws, regulations, policies, and institutions that shut African farmers, especially small farmers, out of the urban centers where consumers are. (Mind you, that's even before you consider the old handicap that has held back agriculture in the region: a land ownership structure that makes it difficult for large agricultural enterprises to set up shop and deploy the kind of modern technology and equipment that small, individual farmers can rarely access.) The entire way from the farm to the kitchen table, red tape, monopolies, and corruption block food trade within Africa, even within each African country. Here is how.

First, each country has its own system to certify seeds, and it takes, on average, a couple of years to approve new varieties. Result: better seeds get stuck at the border, and local farmers are stuck with lower yields—and sometimes without any seeds at all. Something similar is true for fertilizers, which in Burundi, Nigeria, or Senegal can be five times more expensive than in Argentina, India, or Turkey. To make matters worse, some African governments give away fertilizers or sell them below cost. Generous as that may sound, these schemes have mostly turned into political and fiscal nightmares, as waste and corruption make them virtually unaffordable.

Then comes the problem of carrying products to the market. In Africa, it can cost ten times more than in the average rich country to transport one ton of food one kilometer. Much of this is simply due to a lack of adequate roads—the need for investment is enormous. But much also is due to monopolistic—and usually politically connected—trucking companies and "informal" checkpoints—from Cameroon to Kenya, governments struggle to keep locals from setting up roadblocks and charging tolls. Is there any African country that has managed to cut through this Gordian knot and reduce transport prices? Yes, Rwanda did. Hats off to it.

But once farmers reach the border—if they ever do—their troubles really start. From one week to the next, food exports may be banned or taxed—you may not know until you are about to cross. Or the country you are trying to enter may want you to prove where your products come from, or that they meet a sanitary standard that, you guessed it, is different from the one you had to meet back home. They may just want a bribe that would wipe out your by now meager profit. Or they may bluntly abuse their authority. How badly? Half of female cross-border traders in the Great Lakes region report having been physically or sexually harassed by officials at crossing points—grim odds if you have to cross every week. If there is so much risk, why bother to trade food across countries in the first place? Only large, powerful traders can survive. That's precisely the issue. Uncertainty and graft at customs agencies kill the benefits of food trade for Africa's smaller and poorer farmers, most of whom are women.

This all points to the potential gains from African governments acting *together* to free food trade within the continent—of taking collective action toward integration. A set of rules, standards, and taxes that are stable, predictable, and common across countries would go a long way to convince farmers that investing in food trade makes sense. And imagine the impact that a continent-wide "Charter of Basic Rights for Traders" could have. This is not as easy as it sounds—it took decades for Europe to do it. But it is beginning to happen—keep an eye on COMESA, the Common Market of Eastern and Southern Africa.

By some estimates, lifting barriers to food trade, from the farm to the market, could double Africa's production of cassava and rice; triple maize, millet, and sorghum; and quintuple wheat. Think of how, in just five years, Thailand tripled its exports of cassava to other East Asian countries, and picture that success in African proportions. The region could indeed feed itself. That means higher income for farming families, a more secure food supply for city dwellers, and better opportunities for women. A win-win-win opportunity, which raises the question: Why has it not yet been done? Well, that brings us back to politics.

African governments have for years expressed their support for integration. Summits were held and grand free trade agreements were signed. In some cases, customs unions were created within which people, goods, and money were supposed to circulate unfettered—these unions, on paper, still exist. There has been no lack of commitment in public. In practice, though, little has happened. Like any reform, freeing food trade within Africa will have winners and losers. The latter, which include intermediaries, favored companies, and crooked civil servants, can stop change. The only antidote to this is a mix of enlightened leadership, participatory democracy, and lots of user-friendly information. In other words, it will take time but it will come.

How does one fix Africa's statistics?

How would you feel if you were on an airplane and the pilot made the following announcement: *"This is your captain speaking. I'm happy to report that all of our engines checked fine, we have just climbed to thirty-six thousand feet, will soon reach our cruising speed, and should get to our destination right on time . . . I think. You see, the airline has not invested enough in our flight instruments over the past forty years. Some of them are obsolete, some are inaccurate, and some are just plain broken. So, to be honest with you, I'm not sure how good the engines really are. And I can only estimate our altitude, speed, and location. Apart from that, sit back, relax, and enjoy the ride."* This is, in a nutshell, the story of statistics in Africa. Fueled by its many natural resources, the region has been growing fast, is finally beginning to reduce poverty, and seems headed for success. Or so we think, for there are major problems with its data, problems that call for urgent, game-changing action.

First, we don't really know how big (or small) many African economies are. In about half of them, the system of "national accounts" dates back to the 1960s (1968, to be precise); in the other half, it is from 1993. This means that measuring things like how much is produced, consumed, or invested is done with methods from the times when computers were rare, the Internet did not exist, and nobody spoke about "globalization." That is, the methodology ignores that some industries have disappeared and new ones were born. How badly does this skew the data? Well, to give you an idea, when Ghana used a newer methodology (one that works with an economic structure that resembles more closely the country's current reality) to update its accounts in 2010, it found out that its economy was about 60 percent larger than it had previously thought—and the country instantly became "middle income" in the global ranking. (Old-timers have a neat way to tell when the size of an economy is underestimated in countries with weak institutions: if what the government collects in taxes is equivalent to more than one-fifth of the country's GDP, then the GDP is probably larger than what the official numbers show.)

Second, the latest poverty counts for Africa are, on average, five years old. So we only have guesstimates of how the global financial, food, and fuel crises have impacted the distribution of income, wealth, and opportunities in the region. This is because, to count the poor, you need "household surveys"—those face-to-face, home visits where people are asked how much they earn, own, know, and so on. In fifteen African countries, this has been done only once since 2000. Ironically, technology now allows for the surveys to be done not only more frequently but also *continuously*. You give families a cell phone free of charge in exchange for them answering a questionnaire, say, twice a month. And you don't need to ask every household; about three thousand are enough— that's the beauty of statistical sampling. So, why is it not done? Coming to that in a minute.

Third, "industrial" surveys are even more infrequent than household surveys—only a handful of African countries have done at least one in the last ten years. This is a pity. Knowing what your producers are doing—and what keeps them from producing more—is critical if you want to design policies that increase employment, productivity, and economic growth. To be sure, academics, NGOs, development banks, and business organizations carry out sporadic surveys of enterprises for one purpose or another—from understanding how informal jobs are created to selling logistical services.[11] But regular, comprehensive, nationwide data is, at best, rare. What's true for African employers is also true for African employees. "Labor market" surveys are few and far between—most workers, remember, are informal and tend to shy away from answering questions from public officials. So when you ask about the unemployment rate in Africa, you are likely to be given a number that means little, is old, or both.

And how about the good old census—that once-in-a-while count of a country's entire population? Censuses are the only time when we learn how many we are, how fast we are aging, where we live, how we live, and lots of other information that helps governments make smart(er) decisions on things like healthcare, school construction, or crime prevention. Experts say that you should have a census every ten years. Sixteen African countries have fallen behind that tempo—which means that, at the moment, we don't know much about one-third of those who live in the region. Counting people is particularly important in African countries that receive income from extracting oil, gas, or minerals, which is most of them. That income is supposed to be shared among provinces, counties, and municipalities on the basis of their population size—how that's done in practice if the data is outdated or wrong beats a statistician's guess.

How does one even start tackling a problem like that? The truth is that a lot of money has been invested in improving Africa's statistics. Most of that money came as donations from well-meaning rich countries and went to fund "institutional development," that is, to train and equip national statistics offices. According to the "Partnership in Statistics for Development in the 21st Century" (aka PARIS21), between 2009 and 2013 alone, Africa received about 1.5 *billion* dollars to build up its capacity to collect data.[12] That led to some progress, but dismally short of what is needed. Why? Mostly politics. Solution? A mix of democracy and technology.

It is much more difficult to mess with a country's statistics when people are free to complain about it. Democratization has brought a new appetite for information to the average African citizen, much of it expressed through a data-hungry media. The number of recalcitrant governments that gather data but refuse to release it, or release it late when it is obsolete, is falling—slowly but surely. There is even talk of inviting independent experts ("high-level technical commissions") to regularly vet whatever official figures are put out. And the legal walls that protect public statisticians from meddling politicians are hardening—Senegal pioneered the trend in the early 2000s. This is good because national statistics offices are like central banks: once you recruit the best technicians, you want to step back and let them do their job.

But what will really revolutionize African statistics is communication technology. The continent is embracing cellular telephony with gusto; it is only a question of time before its people can become regular respondents in censuses and surveys. (Disclaimer: this writer worked with a team that is trying to do just that through a project beautifully code named "Listening to Africa.") Satellite imagery can now be used to literally see and gauge, from outer space, economic activity in ports, highways, and markets.[13] And tracking what people do, search, or talk about on the Web—their "data exhaust"—gives you a sense of what they are up to as workers, consumers, and investors.[14] All this is yet to be deployed in Africa. To fix its data problem, the region should not just bring up to par the statistical systems it currently has, it may also want to leapfrog into tomorrow's systems.

Did debt forgiveness work in Africa?

When countries in sub-Saharan Africa (which we are calling Africa) gained independence in the 1960s, they inherited little or no public debt. And they stayed relatively debt free until the early 1980s. Then, they went on a borrowing binge. By the mid-1990s, the average nation in the region owed more than the value of all the goods and services it could produce in a year. The loans, which had to be paid back in foreign currency, came mostly from foreign governments and multilateral institutions, not from private bankers. The money was to build things like roads, ports, and power plants; this would speed up economic development and create the capacity to repay. It sounded sensible.

Well, that capacity to repay never really materialized. Corruption, natural disasters, wars, bad policies, and bad luck made it impossible for African governments to keep up with debt payments without cutting basic services to their people, who were already poor and receiving few services in the first place. The image of rich countries forcing poor ones to cut down on schools and hospitals became a political embarrassment, and calls for loan modification proliferated. Creditors came together, financial experts were hired, and African countries got softer deals—"terms," in the jargon—that carried the names of the cities where they were put together—Cologne, Naples, Paris, Toronto, Venice. But that "relief" was not enough. By the early 2000s, the chorus of voices asking for outright debt forgiveness had grown louder—these were the times when NGOs, celebrities, and rock singers started to hold hands with development practitioners. The fact that much of the borrowing had been done behind closed doors by dictators added a moral flavor to the cause.

So, one by one, over the past fifteen years, thirty African countries have seen their debts almost entirely forgiven. Rich countries, the World Bank, the IMF, the African Development Bank—everyone has chipped in. They signed agreements to give up their claims together. (If you work in development, you have probably heard of HIPC—the Heavily Indebted Poor Countries initiative—and MDRI—the Multilateral Debt Relief Initiative.) History does not have many examples of better international collaboration. But, with the process now coming to an end, the final cost of debt relief has become clear: over a hundred billion dollars. So it is fair to ask: Did it work?

In a chapter written for the 2015 *Oxford Handbook of Africa and Economics*, Mark R. Thomas and this writer argue that it did—better than anyone had expected and for a reason that nobody had predicted.[15] Here is why. To qualify for a write-off, countries had to meet four conditions: produce a periodic "Poverty Reduction Strategy Paper" of their own and stick to it, manage the economy well, stay away from expensive borrowing, and put whatever they saved in debt payments into social programs. And they had to do all this transparently—their plans, accounts, and performance were open to all those who had called for debt cancellation.

The visible result of debt forgiveness was indeed a rise in "poverty-reducing expenditures," in some cases by a factor of three. (It is not trivial to define what those expenditures are, but think of them as basic healthcare, primary education, and nutrition programs.) With so many eyes looking, governments did allocate more of their budgets to help poor people.

More subtly, the discipline brought about by the process to qualify for a debt write-off—a discipline that was new for Africa—came in handy when, starting in the mid-2000s, the prices of oil, gas, and minerals began to climb and the technologies to look for natural resources got better and cheaper. Suddenly, African governments had much more money to spend, and new offers to borrow—this time from private bankers. They could have gone on a borrowing binge again. So far, they haven't. In fact, the data shows that, by 2012, countries that had their debts forgiven had better economic policies than the rest of the developing world.[16]

With no choking debt, better management, and rising commodity revenue, Africa has grown faster and for longer than it ever did before—about 5 percent per year in the ten years through 2015. The proportion of Africans living in poverty has been falling for more than a decade. The region even breezed through the global recession of 2009. Sure, it still faces huge challenges, from dismal social services and a paralyzing lack of infrastructure to endemic conflicts and chronic graft. But cautious optimism is in order.

Is that it? Should the old lenders who gave up their claims call it a success and disengage? Hopefully not. As their economies grow, African governments will have easier access to the global financial market—a dozen or so of them already sell bonds abroad. They will enter complex contracts to fund projects and extract even more natural resources. They will be tempted to make promises and give guarantees. Their states and large cities will do some borrowing of their own. This is all normal for up-and-coming developing countries. It just needs to be handled with care and by professionals. That is why those who once pushed for Africa's debt to be forgiven should now push for its capacity to manage future debts to be improved. Rock concerts will never be themed around helping Africa train its civil servants in borrowing strategies, debt accounting, loan auditing, cash-flow forecasting, or data reporting. There is no glamour in good debt management. Alas, that's what the continent urgently needs.

CONCLUDING THOUGHTS

Through questions and answers, this book has brought to you the issues actually faced by those working on economic development. Implicit across those answers were a number of broad messages. Politics can make reforms difficult if not impossible, no matter how sensible and beneficial those reforms may be. Voters' feelings can eclipse policymakers' reasons—Brexit, the revival of populism, and the new voices against globalization attest to that. Being technically right is not enough for change to happen. We know a lot more than before about what works and what doesn't, but at the same time, there are lots of things we still don't know. Risk and uncertainty are the norm. Trial and error and common sense are more useful than scientific sophistication. The main tenets of economic efficiency, social solidarity, public transparency, and environmental sustainability are difficult to quarrel with but are far from universally practiced.

Despite all that, you were also told that we are witnessing, or are about to witness, major transformations and, yes, major progress. The relationship between governments and people is changing for the better—they are becoming closer to each other. Technology and information have offered us new, powerful tools to help the poor and the excluded. We are getting better at managing the economy, although we are still not very good at preventing financial crises. Barring global turbulence or regional conflict, Africa is finally poised to take off—as long as African countries manage their natural wealth well and their goods, people, and capital are allowed to move freely within the continent.

So, with all that in mind, what do *you* think? The opening overview chapter predicted that, by now, you would be convinced that "economic development—and the poverty reduction that goes with it—has never been more feasible for more countries." Are you convinced? If you are skeptical, here is a list of results that you could monitor over the coming years. First, consider the proportion of the world's people living in extreme poverty (remember? $1.90 a day). If all goes well, that proportion should be in the single digits within the next decade. Second, take socioeconomic inclusion. Is development translating into more economic opportunities for women, youth, and the traditionally disadvantaged? Or has it been captured by elites? Third, there is the quality of public services. Things like public schools and hospitals should get better, mostly because there will be easier ways for people to complain and for governments to listen. Corruption will not disappear, but it should get tougher to make a living off of it. Fourth is global trade and investment. If the world economy remains stable, and more countries manage their economies well, you should see more goods, services, and capital moving across borders. Fifth is the speed of environmental degradation. Subsidies for fuel, electricity, water, food, and other goods linked to scarce natural resources should begin to disappear, and their prices should increase, to reflect the true cost of consuming them. And sixth is Africa. You should expect one or more African countries to become success stories, leaders within their region, and places to which people want to migrate.

Growth, inclusion, governance, globalization, sustainability, and Africa: a pretty tall order, isn't it? It would be especially tall if too many rich countries succumbed to nationalism and protectionism. Well, if there is anything you learned from this book, it is that optimism is at the core of the development profession.

NOTES

Overview

1. There are many actors in economic development. Naturally, there are the people who are supposed to benefit from it and, increasingly, are leading it. There are governments, with their public policies and investments. There are official donors, that is, rich countries and their development agencies (like the US Agency for International Development or the UK's Department for International Development). There are local and international nongovernment organizations, many of them focused on specific problems (say, child mortality or barriers to trade). A similar job is done by global private foundations through their large financial endowments (think of the work of the Bill and Melinda Gates Foundation in the fight against malaria). Multilateral development banks, like the World Bank or the African Development Bank, finance long-term projects and give technical advice. The International Monetary Fund helps countries deal with short-term macroeconomic problems. The United Nations' specialized agencies lead international efforts on behalf of, among others, children (UNICEF), refugees (UNHCR), and women (UN WOMEN). There are specialized global funds, to which many of the above contribute money and expertise for a particular cause, like the Global Fund for Children's Vaccines. And finally, there is the universe of academia, think tanks, independent experts, and the media that provide research, ideas, consulting services, and communication.

2. To come up with dollar values that can be compared across countries, we use something called "purchasing power parity" exchange rates, a way to control for differences in prices between each country and the United States. Monetary figures are in US dollars unless otherwise indicated.

Chapter 1

1. You can access the actual revenue information and learn more about EITI at http://www.eiti.org.
2. Leßmann (2006), available online at http://ideas.repec.org/p/ces/ifowps/_25.html.
3. For the classic paper on the risks of decentralization, read Prud'Homme (1994). Available online at http://bit.ly/Yq7MFX. For managing subnational credit and default risks, see Liu and Waibel (2010). Available online at http://bit.ly/15IArne.
4. Iimi (2005). Available online at http://bit.ly/16S9Ebm.
5. Von Braun and Grote (2000). Available online at http://bit.ly/16bh2xd.
6. Ahmad, Brosio, and Tanzi (2008). Available online at http://bit.ly/11Av9xo.
7. Faguet (2004). Available online at http://bit.ly/11zElhy.
8. Garcia and Rajkumar (2008). Available online at http://bit.ly/15IFYtM.
9. Giugale and Webb (2000). Available online at http://bit.ly/14htKfo.
10. To stay up-to-date on the latest research, data, and conferences on fiscal decentralization, visit the website of the World Bank's Global Expert Team on Decentralization: http://www.world-bank.org/publicfinance/decentralization.
11. To find out how the Corruption Perception Index is put together, go to http://www.transparency.org.
12. You can download the 2011 *World Development Report* for free from http://wdr2011.worldbank.org.
13. Many specialized international organizations publish country rankings in their field of expertise. See, for example, http://www.oecd.org for international comparisons of educational achievements, and http://www.freedomhouse.org for comparisons of political and civil rights.
14. Barma, Kaiser, Le, and Vinuela (2012). To read the book online, go to http://bit.ly/rSOxTG.
15. If you want to know more about how Alaska did it, go to http://www.apfc.org.
16. You can check whether your country does at http://www.eiti.org.
17. For plenty of data and information on sovereign wealth funds, check http://www.swfinstitute.org.

Chapter 2

1. Rachel and Smith (2015). Available at http://bit.ly/1SKn56t.
2. For the latest evidence and a synthesis of the literature on this, see IMF (2015).
3. Ibid.
4. An early version of this essay was co-authored with Otaviano Canuto and is based on our 2010 book *The Day after Tomorrow: A Handbook on the Future of Economic Policy in the Developing World*, Washington, DC: World Bank. To download the book for free, visit http://go.worldbank.org/TPPWANWXR0.
5. Feyen et al. (2015). You can download the paper for free at http://bit.ly/2ckpPGq.
6. Sirkeci et al. (2012). Read for free at http://bit.ly/2ckUAuQ.
7. An early version of this essay was co-authored with Otaviano Canuto and is based on our 2010 book *The Day after Tomorrow: A Handbook on the Future of Economic Policy in the Developing World*, Washington, DC: World Bank. To download the book for free, visit http://go.worldbank.org/TPPWANWXR0.
8. Ibid.
9. Ghani ed. (2010b). Read and download for free at http://bit.ly/QGKunz.
10. For an interesting, short article on 3D printing, see *The Economist*, February 10, 2011, http://www.economist.com/node/18114327.
11. OECD (2015).

Chapter 3

1. Piketty (2014).
2. Stiglitz (2015).
3. See an interview with one of those debunkers in *The Economist* online http://www.economist.com/blogs/freeexchange/2015/03/wealth-inequality.
4. See an interesting analysis by Oxfam at https://www.oxfam.org/en/pressroom/pressreleases/2015-01-19/richest-1-will- own-more-all-rest-2016.
5. Cingano (2014).
6. Ostry et al. (2014).
7. Paes de Barros et al. (2009).
8. Greenwood et al. (2014).
9. Eika et al. (2014).

10. You can download the World Development Indicators for free from http://data.worldbank.org/data-catalog/world-development-indicators.

11. Keep in mind that, to make these dollars comparable across countries, they are adjusted by something called "purchasing power parity" exchange rates, that is, by the difference in prices between each country and the United States. Further, the "PPP dollars" are also adjusted for inflation to reflect constant 2011 prices.

12. For an excellent report on conditional cash-transfer programs around the world, see Fiszbein et al. (2009). You can read and download their book for free at http://bit.ly/x17CwG.

13. For a full suite of information on the Human Opportunity Index (books, data, methodology, etc.), visit http://www.worldbank.org/lacopportunity.

14. For a full survey of which governments publish which budget data, something called the "Open Budget Index," visit http://internationalbudget.org/what-we-do/open-budget-survey/rankings-key-findings/rankings/.

15. For a great manual with the latest methodologies for impact evaluation, see Gertler et al. (2011). You can read and download their book for free at http://bit.ly/qV5M12.

Chapter 4

1. You can find an excellent collection of papers on this topic at http://bit.ly/NCGBBr.

2. For papers available online, documenting how women spend more on food than men in Ghana and in Brazil, and more on children's education in China and India, see, respectively, Doss (2006) http://jae.oxfordjournals.org/content/15/1/149.full.pdf+html; Thomas (1990) http://www.jstor.org/stable/145670; Li and Wu (2011) http://qje.oxfordjournals.org/content/123/3/1251.full.pdf+html; and Luke and Munshi (2010) http://www.econ.brown.edu/fac/Kaivan_Munshi/munshi%20&%20luke%20JDE%202010.pdf.

3. World Bank (2012b).

4. Chattopadhyay and Duflo (2004); Iyer et al. (2012); Beaman et al. (2012).

5. Ali et al. (2014).

6. Bandiera et al. (2014).

7. Woodruff and McKenzie (2012).

8. This essay was coauthored with Markus Goldstein.
9. Björkman and Svensson (2009). Available at http://bit.ly/11zSEmo.
10. See the work that Dan Posner and his colleagues have done in Kenya at http://web.mit.edu/posner/www/.
11. Banerjee et al. (2010). Available at http://dspace.mit.edu/handle/1721.1/70931.
12. You ought to watch that short movie. You can find it at https://www.youtube.com/watch?v=z-BQ_NFyeog.
13. You can watch for free a wonderful set of easy-to-understand lectures on behavioral economics, by some of its most advanced practitioners, at http://go.worldbank.org/I1YH87EEQ0.
14. Perry et al. (2007). Available at http://bit.ly/YBsAEw.
15. Benjamin and Mbaye (2012). Available at http://bit.ly/M0mr3u.
16. World Bank (2012d). Available at http://worldbank.org/sar/jobs.
17. Check two reports on informality in the Middle East: World Bank (2009b), available at http://bit.ly/16SkKgr; and Gatti et al. (2011), available at http://bit.ly/2c962dY.

Chapter 5

1. You can read a great 2013 blog by Otaviano Canuto on Brazil's quest for technological upgrading at http://huff.to/X5rpN3.
2. See Dinh, Palmade, Chandra, and Cossar (2012). Available at http://bit.ly/Igem5P.
3. See Farole and Winkler (2014). Available at https://openknowledge.worldbank.org/handle/10986/16390
4. See Im and Rosenblatt (2013). Available at https://openknowledge.worldbank.org/handle/10986/16045
5. Phelps (2013).
6. Rentfrow (2010).
7. Kilroy et al. (2015).
8. You can follow the Allison Park saga at http://saveallisonpark.com/.
9. A good example of this cross-country metrics is the Logistics Performance Index; you can find it at http://bit.ly/8EM7Wf.
10. Coenen et al. (2012); Ellis (2010).
11. World Bank (2014).
12. You can find out more about the initiative, and about the Netherlands' Center for Media and Health that pioneered it, at http://www.media-health.nl.

13. Erten and Ocampo (2012). You can find their paper at http://www.un.org/esa/desa/papers/2012/wp110_2012.pdf.

14. Deaton (2013).

15. Waldron (2007).

16. Giugale and Nguyen (2014).

17. You can learn more about the Sustainable Development Goals at https://sustainabledevelopment.un.org.

18. Three joint documents by developed and developing countries may be useful here: the Paris Declaration of 2005; the Accra Agenda for Action of 2008; and the Busan Partnership of 2011. You can find them all at http://www.oecd.org/dac/effectiveness.

19. To track how this debt relief initiative is going among highly indebted poor countries (HIPCs), go to http://www.imf.org/external/np/exr/facts/hipc.htm.

Chapter 6

1. Much of the slowdown in Africa's growth in 2016 was due to the poor economic performance of its two largest countries: Nigeria and South Africa.

2. This estimate has been produced by Justin Lin (2011a). Available at http://blogs.worldbank.org/developmenttalk/node/646.

3. The book, called *Defragmenting Africa*, was edited by Paul Brenton and Gozde Isik (2012). You can download it for free from http://bit.ly/zjPm4w.

4. If you want to learn more about Nollywood, go to http://newsreel.org/video/THIS-IS-NOLLYWOOD.

5. See Dinh et al. (2012). Available at http://bit.ly/Igem5P.

6. Here is a short blog by Justin Lin describing how that estimate came about: http://blogs.worldbank.org/developmenttalk/how-to-seize-the-85-million-jobs-bonanza.

7. Dinh et al. (2012).

8. Rodrik (2016).

9. Dihel and Goswami (2016). You can download the book for free at http://bit.ly/2ccc0vu.

10. See World Bank (2012a). Available online at http://bit.ly/14D4Cw8.

11. Here you will find a good inventory of those surveys: http://www.enterprisesurveys.org/.

12. Get more information on PARIS21 at http://paris21.org/Press.

13. Henderson, Storeygard, and Weil (2012). Available at http://www.nber.org/papers/w15199.
14. Here is a good blog to get an idea of how "data exhaust" works: http://www.unglobalpulse.org/blog/new-data-landscape.
15. Giugale and Thomas (2015).
16. You can find data on the quality of Africa's institutions and policies at http://datatopics.worldbank.org/cpia/.

BIBLIOGRAPHY

Acemoglu, Daron, Simon Johnson, and James A. Robinson. 2001. "The Colonial Origins of Comparative Development: An Empirical Investigation." *American Economic Review* 91 (5): 1369–1401.

Aghion, Philippe, and Jeffrey G. Williamson. 1998. *Growth, Inequality and Globalization: Theory, History, and Policy*. New York: Cambridge University Press.

Ahmad, Ehtisham, Giorgio Brosio, and Vtio Tanzi. 2008. "Local Service Provision in Selected OECD Countries: Do Decentralized Operations Work Better?" IMF Working Papers WP/08/67. Washington, DC: IMF.

Akerlof, George A., and Rachel E. Kranton. 2010. *Identity Economics: How Our Identities Shape Our Work, Wages, and Well-Being*. Princeton, NJ: Princeton University Press.

Akerlof, George A., and Robert J. Shiller. 2015. *Phishing for Phools: The Economics of Manipulation & Deception*. Princeton, NJ: Princeton University Press.

Ali, Daniel Ayalew, Klaus Deininger, and Markus Goldstein. 2014. "Environmental and Gender Impacts of Land Tenure Regularization in Africa: Pilot Evidence from Rwanda." *Journal of Development Economics* 110 (Sept.): 262–275.

Bandiera, Oriana, Niklas Buehren, Robin Burgess, Markus Goldstein, Selim Gulesci, Imran Rasul, and Munshi Sulaiman. 2014. "Women's Empowerment in Action: Evidence from a Randomized Control Trial in Africa." Economic Organization and Public Policy Discussion Papers Series 50. London: Suntory and Toyota International Centers for Economics and Related Disciplines.

Banerjee, Abhijit V., and Esther Duflo. 2011. *Poor Economics: A Radical Rethinking of the Way to Fight Global Poverty*. New York: Public Affairs.

Banerjee, Abhijit V., Rukmini Banerji, Esther Duflo, Rachel Glennerster, and Stuti Khemani. 2010. "Pitfalls of Participatory Programs: Evidence from a Randomized Evaluation in Education in India." *American Economic Journal: Economic Policy* 2 (1): 1–30.

Bardhan, Pranab K. 2010. *Awakening Giants, Feet of Clay: Assessing the Economic Rise of China and India*. Princeton, NJ: Princeton University Press.

Barma, Naazneen H., Kai Kaiser, Tuan Minh Le, and Lorena Vinuela. 2012. *Rents to Riches? The Political Economy of Natural Resource-led Development*. Washington, DC: World Bank.

Barro, Robert J. 2004. *Economic Growth*, 2nd ed. Cambridge, MA: MIT Press.

Barro, Robert J., and Jong-Wha Lee. 2010. "A New Data Set of Educational Attainment in the World, 1950–2010." Working Paper Series 15902. Cambridge, MA: National Bureau of Economic Research.

Baumol, William J. 2010. *The Microtheory of Innovative Entrepreneurship*. Princeton, NJ: Princeton University Press.

Beaman, Lori, Esther Duflo, Rohini Pande, and Petia Topalova. 2012. "Female Leadership Raises Aspirations and Educational Attainment for Girls: A Policy Experiment in India." *Science* 335 (6068): 582–586.

Benjamin, Nancy, and Ahmadou Aly Mbaye. 2012. *The Informal Sector in Francophone Africa: Firm Size, Productivity and Institutions*. Washington, DC: World Bank.

Bhagwati, Jagdish, and T. N. Srinivasan. 2002. "Trade and Poverty in the Poor Countries." *American Economic Review* 92 (2): 180–183.

Björkman, Martina, and Jacob Svensson. 2009. "Power to the People: Evidence from a Randomized Field Experiment on Community-Based Monitoring in Uganda." *Quarterly Journal of Economics* 124 (2): 735–769.

Bourguignon, François, and Satya Chakravarty. 2003. "The Measurement of Multidimensional Poverty." *Journal of Economic Inequality* 1 (1): 25–49.

Brenton, Paul, and Gozde Isik, eds. 2012. *Defragmenting Africa: Deepening Regional Integration in Goods and Services*. Washington, DC: World Bank.

Canuto, Otaviano, and Marcelo Giugale, eds. 2010. *The Day after Tomorrow: A Handbook on the Future of Economic Policy in the Developing World*. Washington, DC: World Bank.

Chattopadhyay, Raghabendra, and Esther Duflo. 2004. "Women as Policy Makers: Evidence from a Randomized Policy Experiment in India." *Econometrica* 72 (5): 1409–1443.

Cimoli, Mario, Giovanni Dosi, and Joseph E. Stiglitz, eds. 2009. *Industrial Policy and Development: The Political Economy of Capabilities Accumulation*. Oxford: Oxford University Press.

Cingano, F. 2014. "Trends in Income Inequality and Its Impact on Economic Growth." OECD Social, Employment and Migration Working Papers, No. 163. Paris: OECD.

Coenen, Günter, Christopher J. Erceg, Charles Freedman, Davide Furceri, Michael Kumhof, René Lalonde, Douglas Laxton, Jesper Lindé, Annabelle Mourougane, Dirk Muir, Susanna Mursula, Carlos de Resende, John Roberts, Werner Roeger, Stephen Snudden, Mathias Trabandt, and Jan in't Veld. 2012. "Effects of Fiscal Stimulus in Structural Models." *American Economic Journal: Macroeconomics* 4 (1): 22–68.

Collier, Paul. 2007. *The Bottom Billion: Why the Poorest Countries Are Failing, and What Can Be Done about It?* New York: Oxford University Press.

Commission on Growth and Development. 2008. *The Growth Commission Report: Strategies for Sustained Growth and Inclusive Development*. Washington, DC: Commission on Growth and Development.

Cunha, Flavio, James J. Heckman, and Susanne Schennach. 2010. "Estimating the Technology of Cognitive and Noncognitive Skill Formation." *Econometrica* 78 (3): 883–931.

Deaton, Angus. 2013. *The Great Escape: Health, Wealth, and the Origins of Inequality*. Princeton, NJ: Princeton University Press.

Deaton, Angus, and Guy Laroque. 2003. "A Model of Commodity Prices after Sir Arthur Lewis." *Journal of Development Economics* 71: 289–310.

De Soto, Hernando. 1989. *The Other Path: The Invisible Revolution in the Third World*. New York: Harper & Row.

Dihel, Nora, and Arti Grover Goswami. 2016. *The Unexplored Potential of Trade in Services in Africa: From Hair Stylists and Teachers to Accountants and Doctors*. Washington, DC: World Bank.

Dinh, Hinh T., Vincent Palmade, Vandana Chandra, and Frances Cossar. 2012. *Light Manufacturing in Africa: Targeted Policies to Enhance Private Investment and Create Jobs*. Washington, DC: World Bank and L'Agence Française de Développement.

Doss, Cheryl. 2006. "The Effects of Intra-household Property Ownership on Expenditure Patterns in Ghana." *Journal of African Economies* 15 (1): 149–180.

Easterly, William. 2002. *The Elusive Quest for Growth: Economists' Adventures and Misadventures in the Tropics*. Cambridge, MA: MIT Press.

Easterly, William. 2006. *The White Man's Burden: Why the West's Efforts to Aid the Rest Have Done So Much Ill and So Little Good*. New York: Penguin.

Eika, Lasse, Magne Mogstad, and Basit Zafar. 2014. "Educational Assortative Mating and Household Income Inequality." Federal Reserve Bank of New York Staff Reports 682. New York: Federal Reserve Bank.

Ellis, Jennifer. 2010. "The Effects of Fossil-Fuel Subsidy Reform: A Review of Modelling and Empirical Studies." Social Science Research Network No. 1572397.

Erten, Bilge, and Jose Antonio Ocampo. 2012. "Supercycles of Commodity Prices since the Mid-nineteenth Century." DESA Working Paper 110. New York: UN-DESA.

Farole, Thomas, and Deborah Winkler. 2014. *Making Foreign Direct Investment Work for Sub-Saharan Africa: Local Spillovers and Competitiveness in Global Value Chains*. Directions in Development—Trade. Washington, DC: World Bank.

Faguet, Jean-Paul. 2004. "Does Decentralization Increase Government Responsiveness to Local Needs? Evidence from Bolivia." *Journal of Public Economics* 88 (3–4): 867–893.

Feyen, Erik H. B., Swati R. Ghosh, Katie Kibuuka, and Subika Farazi. 2015. "Global Liquidity and External Bond Issuance in Emerging Markets and Developing Economies." Policy Research Working Paper Number WPS 7363. Washington, DC: World Bank.

Fields, Gary. 2011. *Working Hard, Working Poor*. New York: Oxford University Press.

Fischer, Stanley. 1993. "The Role of Macroeconomic Factors in Growth." *Journal of Monetary Economics* 32 (3): 485–512.

Fiszbein, Ariel, Norbert Schady, Francisco H. G. Ferreira, Margaret Grosh, Nial Kelleher, Pedro Olinto, and Emmanuel Skoufias. 2009.

Conditional Cash Transfers: Reducing Present and Future Poverty.
Washington, DC: World Bank.

Fitoussi, Jean-Paul, Amartya Sen, and Joseph E. Stiglitz.
2010. *Mismeasuring Our Lives: Why GDP Doesn't Add Up.*
New York: New Press.

Fogel, Robert. 1999. "Catching Up with the Economy." *American Economic Review* 89 (1) (Mar.): 1–21.

Foster, Vivien, and Cecilia Briceño-Garmendia, eds. 2010.
Africa's Infrastructure: A Time for Transformation. Washington,
DC: World Bank.

Fukuyama, Francis. 1995. *Trust: The Social Virtues and the Creation of Prosperity.* New York: Free Press.

Garcia, Marito, and Charity M. T. Moore. 2012. *The Cash Dividend: The Rise of Cash Transfer Programs in Sub-Saharan Africa.* Washington,
DC: World Bank.

Garcia, Marito, and Andrew Sunil Rajkumar. 2008. *Achieving Better Service Delivery through Decentralization in Ethiopia.* Washington,
DC: World Bank.

Gatti, Roberta, Diego Angel-Urdinola, Joana Silva, and Andras Bodor.
2011. *Striving for Better Jobs: The Challenge of Informality in the Middle East and North Africa.* Washington, DC: World Bank.

Gelb, Alan, and Caroline Decker. 2011. "Cash at Your
Fingertips: Biometric Technology for Transfers in Developing and
Resource-Rich Countries." Working Paper Series 253. Washington,
DC: Center for Global Development.

Gertler, Paul J., Sebastian Martinez, Patrick Premand, Laura
B. Rawlings, Christel M. J. Vermeersch. 2011. *Impact Evaluation in Practice.* Washington, DC: World Bank.

Ghani, Ejaz, ed. 2010a. *The Services Revolution in South Asia.*
New York: Oxford University Press.

Ghani, Ejaz, ed. 2010b. *The Poor Half Billion in South Asia.* Washington,
DC: World Bank and Oxford University Press.

Gill, Indermit, and Homi Kharas. 2007. *An East Asian Renaissance: Ideas for Economic Growth.* Washington, DC: World Bank.

Giugale, Marcelo, and Steven Webb, eds. 2000. *Achievements and Challenges in Fiscal Decentralization: Lessons from Mexico.*
Washington, DC: World Bank.

Giugale, Marcelo, and Nga Thi Viet Nguyen. 2014. "Money to the
People: Estimates of the Potential Scale of Direct Dividend Payments
in Africa." Center for Global Development Policy Paper 043.

Giugale, Marcelo, and Mark Thomas. 2015. "African Debt and Debt Relief." In *The Oxford Handbook of Africa and Economics*, ed. Celestin Monga and Justin Yifu Lin, vol. 2, 186–203. New York: Oxford University Press.

Greenwood, Jeremy, Nezih Guner, Georgi Kocharkov, and Cezar Santos. 2014. "Marry Your Like: Assortative Mating and Income Inequality." *American Economic Review* 104 (5): 348–353.

Guasch, J. Luis. 2004. *Granting and Renegotiating Infrastructure Concessions: Doing It Right*. Washington, DC: World Bank.

Hall, Gillette H., and Harry Anthony Patrinos, eds. 2012. *Indigenous Peoples, Poverty and Development*. New York: Cambridge University Press.

Hausmann, Ricardo, and Rodrik, Dani. 2003. "Economic Development as Self-Discovery." *Journal of Development Economics* 72: 603–633.

Hausmann, Ricardo, César Hidalgo, Sebastián Bustos, Michele Coscia, Sarah Chung, Juan Jimenez, Alexander Simoes, and Muhammend A. Yildirim. 2011. *The Atlas of Economic Complexity: Mapping Paths to Prosperity*. Cambridge, MA: Harvard University.

Heckman, James J. 2008. "The Case for Investing in Disadvantaged Young Children." In *Big Ideas for Children: Investing in Our Nation's Future*, 49–58. Washington, DC: First Focus.

Henderson, J. Vernon, Adam Storeygard, and David N. Weil. 2012. "Measuring Economic Growth from Outer Space." *American Economic Review* 102 (2): 994–1028.

Hirschman, Albert O. 1981. "The Changing Tolerance for Income Inequality in the Course of Economic Development." In *Essays in Trespassing*, Cambridge: Cambridge University Press.

Hirschman, Albert O. 1987. "The Political Economy of Latin American Development: Seven Exercises in Retrospection." *Latin American Research Review* 22 (3): 7–36.

Iyer, Lakshmi, Anandi Mani, Prachi Mishra, and Petia Topalova. 2012. "The Power of Political Voice: Women's Political Representation and Crime in India." *American Economic Journal: Applied Economics* 4 (4) : 165–193.

Hoekman, Bernard. 2011. "Aid for Trade: Why, What, and Where Are We?" In *Unfinished Business? The WTO's Doha Agenda*, ed. Will Martin and Aaditya Mattoo, 233–254. London: London Publishing Partnership.

Holden, Stein T., Keijiro Otsuka, and Frank M. Place, eds. 2009. *The Emergence of Land Markets in Africa: Assessing the Impacts on Poverty, Equity, and Efficiency.* Washington, DC: Resources for the Future.

Iimi, Atsushi. 2005. "Decentralization and Economic Growth Revisited: An Empirical Note." *Journal of Urban Economics* 57: 449–461.

Im, Fernando Gabriel, and David Rosenblatt. 2013. "Middle-Income Traps: A Conceptual and Empirical Survey." Policy Research Working Paper No. 6594. Washington, DC: World Bank.

IMF. 2015. "Structural Reforms and Macroeconomic Performance: Initial Considerations for the Fund." IMF Staff Report. Washington, DC: IMF.

Kanbur, Ravi, and Jan Svejnar, eds. 2009. *Labor Markets and Economic Development.* New York: Routledge.

Kharas, Homi, and Wolfgang Fengler, eds. 2010. *Delivering Aid Differently: Lessons from the Field.* Washington, DC: Brookings Institution Press.

Kilroy, Austin Francis Louis, Megha Mukim, and Stefano Negri. 2015. *Competitive Cities for Jobs and Growth: What, Who, and How.* Washington, DC: World Bank.

Klein, Michael U., and Tim Harford. 2005. *The Market for Aid.* Washington, DC: International Finance Corporation.

Krugman, Paul R. 1991a. *Geography and Trade.* Cambridge, MA: MIT Press.

Krugman, Paul R. 1991b. "Increasing Returns and Economic Geography." *Journal of Political Economy* 99 (3): 483–499.

Krugman, Paul R. 2009. "The Increasing Returns Revolution in Trade and Geography." *American Economic Review* 99 (3): 561–571.

Layard, Richard. 2005. *Happiness: Lessons from a New Science.* London: Penguin Press.

Lederman, Daniel, and William F. Maloney. 2012. *Does What You Export Matter? In Search of Empirical Guidance for Industrial Policies.* Washington, DC: World Bank.

Leßmann, Christian. 2006. "Fiscal Decentralization and Regional Disparity: A Panel Data Approach for OECD Countries." Ifo Working Paper Series No. 25. Munich: Ifo Institute for Economic Research at the University of Munich.

Levy, Santiago. 2008. *Good Intentions, Bad Outcomes: Social Policy, Informality, and Economic Growth in Mexico.* Washington, DC: Brookings Institution Press.

Li, Lixing, and Xiaoyu Wu. 2011. "Power and Intra-household Resource Allocation in China." *Journal of Human Resources* 46 (2): 295–316.

Lin, Justin Yifu. 2011a. "How to Seize the 85 Million Jobs Bonanza." World Bank (blog), Washington, DC. http://blogs.worldbank.org/developmenttalk/node/646.

Lin, Justin Yifu 2011b. "From Flying Geese to Leading Dragons: New Opportunities and Strategies for Structural Transformation in Developing Countries." Policy Research Working Papers Series 5702. Washington, DC: World Bank.

Liu, Lili, and Michael Waibel. 2010. "Managing Subnational Credit and Default Risk." Policy Research Working Papers Series 5362. Washington, DC: World Bank.

Lopez-Acevedo, Gladys, Philipp Krause, and Keith Mackay, eds. *Building Better Policies: The Nuts and Bolts of Monitoring and Evaluation Systems*. Washington, DC: World Bank.

Lopez, J. Humberto, and Pablo Fajnzylber, eds. 2008. *Remittances and Development: Lessons from Latin-America*. Washington, DC: World Bank.

Luke, Nancy, and Kaivan Munshi. 2010. "Women as Agents of Change: Female Income and Mobility in India." *Journal of Development Economics* 94 (1): 1–17.

Maddison, Angus. 2007. *Contours of the World Economy, 1–2030 AD*. Oxford: Oxford University Press.

Molinas, Jose R., Ricardo Paes de Barros, Jaime Saavedra, and Marcelo Giugale. 2010. *Do Our Children Have a Chance? The 2010 Human Opportunity Report for Latin America and the Caribbean*. Washington, DC: World Bank.

Moss, Todd J. 2007. *African Development: Making Sense of the Issues and Actors*. Boulder, CO: Lynne Rienner.

Moyo, Dambisa. 2009. *Dead Aid: Why Aid Is Not Working and How There Is a Better Way for Africa*. New York: Penguin.

North, Douglass C. 1990. *Institutions, Institutional Change and Economic Performance*. New York: Cambridge University Press.

North, Douglass C., John J. Wallis, Steven B. Webb, and Barry R. Weingast. 2013. *In the Shadow of Violence: Politics, Economics and the Problems of Development*. New York: Cambridge University Press.

OECD. 2015. *Measuring and Monitoring BEPS, Action 11—2015 Final Report*. Paris: OECD.

Ostrom, Elinor. 1990. *Governing the Commons: The Evolution of Institutions for Collective Action.* Cambridge: Cambridge University Press.

Ostry, Jonathan D., Andrew Berg, and Charalambos G. Tsangarides. 2014. "Redistribution, Inequality, and Growth." IMF Staff Discussion Note 14/02. Washington, DC: IMF.

Paes de Barros, Ricardo, Francisco H. G. Ferreira, José R. Molinas Vega, and Jaime Saavedra Chanduvi. 2009. *Measuring Inequality of Opportunities in Latin America and the Caribbean.* Washington, DC: World Bank.

Pagés, Carmen, ed. 2010. *The Age of Productivity: Transforming Economies from the Bottom Up.* New York: Palgrave Macmillan.

Perry, Guillermo E., William F. Maloney, Omar S. Arias, Pablo Fajnzylber, Andrew D. Mason, and Jaime Saavedra-Chanduvi. 2007. *Informality: Exit and Exclusion.* Washington, DC: World Bank.

Phelps, Edmund. 2013. *Mass Flourishing: How Grassroots Innovation Created Jobs, Challenge, and Change.* Princeton, NJ: Princeton University Press.

Piketty, Thomas. 2014. *Capital in the Twenty-First Century.* Boston: Harvard University Press.

Porter, Michael E. 1990. *The Competitive Advantage of Nations.* New York: Free Press.

Prebisch, Raul. 1950. *The Economic Development of Latin America and Its Principal Problems.* New York: United Nations.

Pritchett, Lant. 2006. *Let Their People Come: Breaking the Gridlock on Global Labor Mobility.* Washington, DC: Center for Global Development.

Prud'Homme, Remmy. 1994. "On the Dangers of Decentralization." Policy Research Working Papers Series 1252. Washington, DC: World Bank.

Rachel, Lukasz, and Thomas D. Smith. 2015. "Secular Drivers of the Global Real Interest Rate." Staff Working Paper No. 571. London: Bank of England.

Ravallion, Martin. 2001. "Growth, Inequality, and Poverty: Looking Beyond Averages." Policy Research Working Paper 2558. Washington, DC: World Bank.

Reinhart, Carmen, and Kenneth Rogoff. 2008. "This Time Is Different! A Panoramic View of Eight Centuries of Financial Crisis." Working Paper 13882. Cambridge, MA: National Bureau of Economic Research.

Rentfrow, P. J. 2010. "Statewide Differences in Personality: Toward a Psychological Geography of the United States." *American Psychologist* 65: 548–558.

Rodrik, Dani. 2004. "Industrial Policy for the Twenty-First Century." Discussion Paper Series 4767. London: Centre for Economic Policy Research.

Rodrik, Dani. 2007. *One Economics, Many Recipes: Globalization, Institutions, and Economic Growth*. Princeton, NJ: Princeton University Press.

Rodrik, Dani. 2016. "Premature Deindustrialization." *Journal of Economic Growth* 21 (1): 1–33.

Roemer, John E. 1998. *Equality of Opportunity*. Cambridge, MA: Harvard University Press.

Romer, Paul. 2010. *Technologies, Rules, and Progress: The Case for Charter Cities*. Washington, DC: Center for Global Development.

Schumpeter, Joseph Alois. 1934. *The Theory of Economic Development: An Inquiry into Profits, Capital, Credit, Interest, and the Business Cycle*. Cambridge, MA: Harvard University Press.

Schumpeter, Joseph Alois. 1939. *Business Cycles*, vols. 1 and 2. New York: McGraw-Hill.

Serven, Luis, and Klaus Schmitt-Hebbel, eds. 1999. *Economics of Savings and Growth*. Cambridge: Cambridge University Press.

Sen, Amartya. 1999. *Development as Freedom*. New York: Knopf.

Sen, Amartya, and Geoffrey Hawthorn. 1987. *The Standard of Living*. Cambridge: Cambridge University Press.

Singer, Peter. 2009. *The Life You Can Save: Acting Now to End World Poverty*. New York: Random House.

Sirkeci, Ibrahim, Jeffrey H. Cohen, and Dilip Ratha. 2012. *Migration and Remittances during the Global Financial Crisis and Beyond*. Washington, DC: World Bank.

Stern, Nicholas. 2007. *The Economics of Climate Change: The Stern Review*. Cambridge: Cambridge University Press.

Stiglitz, Joseph E. 1996. "Some Lessons from the East Asian Miracle." *World Bank Research Observer* 11 (2): 151–177.

Stiglitz, Joseph E. 2015. *The Great Divide—Unequal Societies and What We Can Do about Them*. New York: W. W. Norton.

Thomas, Duncan. 1990. "Intra-Household Resource Allocation: An Inferential Approach." *Journal of Human Resources* 25 (4): 635–664.

United Nations Department of Economic and Social Affairs. 2010. *The World's Women 2010: Trends and Statistics*. New York: United Nations.

United Nations Economic Commission for Europe. 2010. *Measuring Quality of Employment: Country Pilot Reports*. Geneva: United Nations.

United Nations Environment Program. 2011. *Towards a Green Economy: Pathways to Sustainable Development and Poverty Eradication*. Geneva: UNEP.

Von Braun, Joachim, and Ulrike Grote. 2000. "Does Decentralization Serve the Poor?" Mimeo.

Waldron, Hilary. 2007. "Trends in Mortality Differentials and Life Expectancy for Male Social Security-Covered Workers by Socioeconomic Status." *Social Security Bulletin* 67 (3): 1–28.

Wolf, Martin. 2004. *Why Globalization Works*. New Haven, CT: Yale University Press.

Woodruff, Christopher, and David McKenzie. 2012. "Improving the Productivity and Earnings of Women Owned and/or Managed Enterprises in Developing Countries: What Works?" Mimeo.

World Bank. 1992. *World Development Report 1992: Development and the Environment*. New York: Oxford University Press.

World Bank. 1993. *The East Asian Miracle*. Washington, DC: World Bank.

World Bank. 2005. *World Development Report 2006: Equity and Development*. New York: Oxford University Press.

World Bank. 2006. *World Development Report 2007: Development and the Next Generation*. Washington, DC: World Bank.

World Bank. 2008. *Growth Report: Strategies for Sustained Growth and Inclusive Development*. Washington, DC: World Bank.

World Bank. 2009a. *World Development Report 2009: Reshaping Economic Geography*. Washington, DC: World Bank.

World Bank. 2009b. *From Privilege to Competition: Unlocking Private-Led Growth in the Middle East and North Africa*. Washington, DC: World Bank.

World Bank. 2010. *World Development Report 2010: Development and Climate Change*. Washington, DC: World Bank.

World Bank. 2011a. *World Development Report 2011: Conflict, Security, and Development*. Washington, DC: World Bank.

World Bank. 2011b. *More and Better Jobs in South Asia*. Washington, DC: World Bank.

World Bank. 2012a. *Africa Can Help Feed Africa: Removing Barriers to Regional Trade in Food Staples*. Washington, DC: World Bank.

World Bank. 2012b. *World Development Report 2012: Gender Equality and Development*. New York: Oxford University Press.

World Bank. 2012c. *World Development Report 2013: Jobs*. Washington, DC: World Bank.

World Bank. 2012d. *More and Better and Jobs in South Asia.* Washington, DC: World Bank.

World Bank. 2012e. *Inclusive Green Growth—The Pathway to Sustainable Development*. Washington, DC: World Bank.

World Bank. 2013. *Africa Can Help Feed Africa: Removing Barriers to Regional Trade in Food Staples*. Washington, DC: World Bank.

World Bank. 2014. *The Economic Impact of the 2014 Ebola Epidemic: Short and Medium Term Estimates for West Africa*. Report No. 91219. Washington, DC: World Bank.

Yunus, Muhammad, and Alan Jolis. 1999. *Banker to the Poor: Micro-Lending and the Battle against World Poverty*. New York: Public Affairs.

INDEX